CARD
GAMES

Publications International, Ltd.

Cover and interior art: Shutterstock.com

Contributing writers: David Galt, Karolyn A. Schalk, Wesley Young

Louis Weber, CEO
Publications International, Ltd.
7373 North Cicero Avenue
Lincolnwood, Illinois 60712

ISBN: 978-1-68022-129-9

Manufactured in China.

8 7 6 5 4 3 2 1

For more than 600 years, card games have helped people past the time, satisfy their competitive urges, and have fun! In this book, we've assembled card games to suit all tastes and occasions. You'll find games suited for a quiet evening with one or two people or a fun party with a larger group. Some games are easy to learn and great for families, while others are more competitive and will require you to practice and learn skill and strategy.

In the following pages you'll find instructions for some of the most popular card games, including several variations of Poker, Rummy, and Bridge. All the games are carefully and clearly explained so that even inexperienced card players can easily learn to play. You will find rules of play, game objective, suggested number of players, card requirements, and scoring rules. Also included are tips to help you formulate a strategy, as well as variations for modifying games. The rules provided are merely guidelines; once you get the hang of playing, you might just develop your own variations! A handy glossary at the back of the book defines important terms and card-table jargon.

Even if you're an "old hand" at cards, you'll find some games you haven't tried, as well as a few new wrinkles in games you thought you knew well. If you're new to card-playing, this is the place to learn the basics of a large variety of games. Whatever your experience, if you're looking to deal out some fun, this book is your best bet.

♣ ◆ ♠ ♥

CONTENTS

ACEY-DEUCEY

This card game is a popular wagering game. It's also called Yablon, Between the Sheets, and Red Dog (in casinos).

♣ ♦ ♠ ♥

PLAYERS

Two or more with one selected as the banker. All others bet against the banker.

OBJECT

To win the bets you place.

CARDS

Usually four or five decks, all cards shuffled together, known as a shoe. You may play with fewer or more decks. Aces are high.

PLAYING

You'll need a supply of chips and to set a betting limit. Choose a banker, who is also the dealer. Each player bets. Then banker deals two cards face up. The cards apply to all betting players.

If the cards are next to each other in rank (e.g., ♥5, ♦6), all bets are off! Retire those two cards. Players may alter their bet amounts, and dealer turns up two new cards.

If the cards are the same (e.g., two 10s), banker deals up one more card. If it also is the same rank, then banker must pay 11 to 1 on the amounts bet.But if it's any other card, bets again are cancelled, and these three cards are removed.

When the two turned cards have a gap, or spread, in rank (ace high, deuce low), the fun begins. Players who want to may raise their bet up to double their original bet amount. Next, the dealer turns up a third card. If it ranks between the two upcards, the bettors win. But if the third card either matches one of the two upcards or is outside the spread, then the banker wins all bets.

PAYOFF SCHEDULE

When the card turned falls within a spread of 4–11, banker pays each bettor the amount bet—an even payoff.

When the spread is three (e.g., ♣2-♠6), banker pays twice the bets.

When the spread is two (e.g., ♠7-♦4), banker pays four times the bets.

When the spread is one (e.g., ♥A-♥Q), banker pays six times the bets.

Because the banker has a small edge in this game, the role of banker should rotate among the players.

TIP

Acey-Deucey is an easy game to learn, but relies on luck and favors the banker. For that reason, it may work better as a casual party game where people are playing for low stakes, such as pieces of candy instead of money.

The only strategy you can employ in Acey-Deucey is deciding when to increase your bet. Whenever the spread is seven or more (e.g., ♠3-♣J), the odds favor you. When the spread is 6 or less, you're bucking the odds if you increase your bet.

BEZIQUE

Bezique, the forerunner of Pinochle, was invented in the early 1800s in Sweden. By the 1850s, it was a hit all across Europe, and it soon arrived in America. It's still widely enjoyed in Britain.

♣ ♦ ♠ ♥

PLAYERS

Two

OBJECT

To score points by melding and by taking tricks containing aces and 10s (brisques).

CARDS

Two sets of 32 cards, consisting of aces through 7s, are shuffled together into one 64-card deck. Cards rank—from high to low— A-10-K-Q-J-9-8-7.

PLAYING

Deal eight cards to each player (in groups of three, two, and three), and then turn up a card to designate trumps. Place that card face up and so that it is slightly sticking out from under the draw pile. If the trump upcard is a 7, dealer scores 10 points immediately.

Nondealer starts play by leading any card. At this stage of play, and as long as there remain cards to draw, you are not obliged to follow suit and may play any of your cards.

The highest trump in a trick wins it, or, if there is no trump card, the highest card of the suit led wins it. When two identical cards contend for the same trick (for example, two ♥10s), the first one played wins the trick.

The winner of each trick scores 10 points for each ace or 10 (brisque) it contains, and may also table one meld. (You may tally the 10 points for a 7 of trumps along with a meld, and if you table the first 7 of trumps you may also trade it for the trump upcard.) Tally all points when you meld as you score them. Tally brisques at the end of the hand.

Trump marriage (K-Q)	40 points
Non-trump marriage (K-Q in same suit)	20 points
Trump flush (A-10-K-Q-J)	250 points
Bezique (♠Q-♦J)	40 points
Double bezique (♠Q-♦J-♠Q-♦J)	500 points
Any four aces	100 points

Any four kings	80 points
Any four queens	60 points
Any four jacks	40 points
7 of trumps (each)	10 points

Both players take a new card from the stock, with the winner of the previous trick drawing first and then leading to the next trick.

Melded cards stay on the table until the stock is used up, but you may still play them on tricks. A card you meld one time can be used again, but only in a different meld and only with a winning trick. For example: ♣Q melds with ♣K in a marriage and can also meld later for 60 points with ♥Q-♦Q-♠Q. But it can't meld with a second ♣K—a completely new pair is needed to score the second marriage.

When only the upcard and one draw card remain, the upcard goes to the trick-loser. Put your remaining melded cards back in your hand, with the winner of the previous trick taking the last draw card and leading to the next trick. In the play of the final eight cards, each player must follow suit and also must win a trick whenever possible. Whoever wins the final trick scores an extra 10 points.

SCORING

The first player to accumulate 1,000 points—or any other agreed-upon sum—wins.

TIPS

The play in Bezique has 32 tricks, in which your opponent will try to trump any ace or 10 you lead. Therefore, you should save your 10s to win lower cards when your opponent leads. Meanwhile, there's usually a difficult suit for your opponent to win tricks in. Even if you lead low cards of that suit, it may cause discomfort: Players want to hold on to melding cards (aces, kings, queens, the 10 and jack of trumps, and ♠Q and ♦J for a possible 500-point double bezique). Yet each player can hold onto just eight cards!

If you have a big meld near the end of the game—for example, ♠Q-♠Q-♦J-♦J—you may not have time to meld it in two stages to score an extra 40 points. Your opponent may see through that plan and prevent you from winning a second trick and the additional 500 points.

Dealt this hand, you want to win a trick so that you can exchange the ♥7 for the ♥K (pulled out here for clarity), giving you an immediate 40-point trump marriage (♥K-♥Q). You should not play an ace, which would reduce your chance to complete a meld of 4 aces. The ♣10 is a possible lead, though it gives opponent the chance to win a brisque. Instead, you could try either ♠J, but as a card of lower rank, it is a more likely loser.

RUBICON BEZIQUE

Rubicon Bezique became very popular because of its emphasis on melding.

♣ ◆ ♠ ♥

PLAYERS

Two

OBJECT

To attain the better score. Each deal is one game. A losing player scoring under 1,000 points is said to be rubiconed.

CARDS

Two 64-card Bezique decks (128 cards total).

PLAYING

This game is similar to regular Bezique, but deal nine cards instead of eight. The first melded marriage determines the trump suit. There is no trump until a marriage is declared. If you're dealt a carte blanche (no picture cards), show it and score 50, and score 50 more after each draw until you do get a picture card!

SCORING

New melds include triple bezique (1,500 points), quadruple bezique (4,500 points) and backdoor (nontrump A-K-Q-J-10=150 points). A meld can be remade even by replacing a played melded card for a trick!

Although the winner of a trick still gathers the two played cards, brisques (aces and tens) are not scored unless they are needed to break a tie or to allow a player to avoid being rubiconed. If one player counts brisques, both must count them.

Last trick counts 50 points.

The 7 of trumps is not scored.

As with all Bezique games, no declarations are scored after the stock pile is depleted. The player with the highest score at the end of the game adds 500 points. If the loser is rubiconed, the winner of a Rubicon game receives a 1,000-point bonus instead of 500 as well as 320 credit for brisques, plus all the opponent's points!

SIX-PACK BEZIQUE

Six-Pack Bezique, also known as Chinese Bezique, is fast paced and high scoring; it was reportedly Winston Churchill's favorite game.

♣ ♦ ♠ ♥

PLAYERS

Two

OBJECT

To score a high number of points. Each deal is one game. Loser must reach 3,000 points or be rubiconed.

CARDS

Three 64-card Bezique packs (192 cards total).

PLAYING

Players cut to determine dealer, with the choice going to the player with the high card. Cut again if cards are the same rank. It is a disadvantage to be dealer.

Deal 12 cards each. It is common to pile up cards played in tricks on the table, where all can see what's been played. Or you may collect them in a neat pile. Brisques and sevens are not scored. There is no trump until the first marriage determines the trump. That trump remains in the next game until that game's first marriage is declared.

SCORING

If dealer lifts 24 cards from the deck when cutting cards at the outset, dealer scores 250 points. If nondealer guesses the correct number of lifted cards, that player scores 150 points. Carte blanche scores 250, and 250 with each succeeding drawn card that is not a face card. Winning the last trick earns 250. The other melds are scored in subsequent winning tricks. The winner of the game receives an additional 1,000 points. If the loser is rubiconed, the winner scores that additional 1,000 points plus the loser's points.

TIP

Remember, you can score again for a meld just by replacing one card. So after melding four kings, if you play one and can replace it later, you score for the entire meld again. In this way you will not only increase your score, but you might also attain the points needed for game.

MELD SCORES

Meld scores are as in Rubicon Bezique, with these additional scores:

Four aces of trump	1,000		Four queens of trump	600
Four tens of trump	900		Four jacks of trump	400
Four kings of trump	800			

BLACKJACK

Blackjack is a favorite of high rollers and amateurs alike.
With a few simple strategies, you can elevate your game.

♣ ♦ ♠ ♥

PLAYERS

A dealer and up to seven players

OBJECT

To draw cards totaling closer to 21 than the dealer's cards without going over that number. The best total is a two-card 21, or a Blackjack.

CARDS

One or more standard 52-card decks, with each denomination assigned a point value.

The cards 2 through ten are worth their face value. Kings, queens, and jacks are each worth 10, and aces may be used as either 1 or 11.

PLAYING

At a casino, the game is usually played at an arc-shaped table with places for up to seven players on the outside and for the dealer on the inside. At one corner of the table is a rectangular placard that tells the minimum and maximum bets at that table, as well as giving variations in common rules. For example, the sign might say, "BLACKJACK. $5 to $2,000. Split any pair three times. Double on any two cards." That means the minimum bet at this table is $5 and the maximum is $2,000. Pairs may be split according to the rules described later, and if more matching cards are dealt, the pairs may be split up to three times for a total of four hands. The player may double the original bet (double down) and receive just one more card on any two-card total.

Most games today use four, six, or eight decks. After being shuffled, the cards are placed in a receptacle called a "shoe," from which the dealer can slide out one card at a time. Single- or double-deck games may be dealt from the dealer's hand. Play begins when you place a bet by stacking a chip or chips in the betting square on the table directly in front of you. After all bets have been placed, each player and the dealer are given two cards. In a shoe game, all player cards are dealt faceup, and the players are not permitted to touch their cards. In a single- or double-deck game dealt by hand, cards are dealt facedown and players may pick them up with one hand. Either way, one of the dealer's cards is turned faceup so the players can see it.

Once the cards have been dealt, players decide in turn how to play out their hands. After all players have finished, the dealer must play his/her hand according to set rules: The dealer must draw more cards to any total of 16 or less and must stand on any total of 17 or more. In some casinos, the dealer will also draw to "soft" 17—a 17 including an ace or aces that could also be counted as a 7. The most common soft 17 is A-6, but several other totals, such as A-3-3 or A-4-2, on up to A-A-A-A-A-A-A in a multiple deck game, are soft 17s.

HIT

If you hit, you take another card or cards in the hope of getting closer to 21. If the player's total exceeds 21 after hitting, the player is said to "bust" and loses the bet. In shoe games, the player signals a hit by pointing to his cards or scratching or waving toward himself. In facedown games, the player signals a hit by scratching the table with the cards. Verbal calls to hit are not accepted—hand signals are used for the benefit of the security cameras above the table, so a taped record is available to settle any potential disputes.

STAND

If you stand, you elect to draw no more cards in the hope that the current total will beat the dealer. Signal a stand by holding a flattened palm over your cards in a faceup game or by sliding your cards under your bet in a facedown game.

It is a good idea to stand with hands totaling between 17 and 20.

DOUBLE DOWN

You may elect to double your original bet and receive only one more card regardless of its denomination. Some casinos restrict doubling down to hands in which your first two cards total 10 or 11. Others allow you to double on any two cards. Double down by taking a chip or chips equal to the amount of your original bet and placing it next to your bet. At this point in a facedown game, you also need to turn your two original cards faceup.

You can double down on hands like these totaling 10 or 11.

SPLIT

If your first two cards are the same denomination, you may elect to make a second bet equal to your first and split the pair, using each card as the first card in a separate hand. For example, if you are dealt two 8s, you may slide a second bet equal to the first into your betting box. The dealer will separate the 8s, then put a second card on the first 8. You play out that hand in normal fashion until you either stand or bust; then the dealer puts a second card on the second 8, and you play out that hand.

INSURANCE

If the dealer's faceup card is an ace, you may take "insurance," which is essentially a bet that the dealer has a 10-value card face-down to complete a Blackjack. Insurance, which may be taken for half the original bet, pays 2–1 if the dealer has Blackjack. The net effect is that if you win the insurance bet and lose the hand, you come out even. For example, a player has 18 with a $10 bet down. The dealer has an ace up. The player takes a $5 insurance bet. If the dealer has Blackjack, the player loses the $10 bet on the hand but wins $10 with the 2–1 pay off on the $5 insurance bet. Generally, taking insurance is a bad percentage play, no matter what the player total, unless the player is a card counter who knows that an unusually large concentration of 10-value cards remains to be played.

ETIQUETTE

When you sit down at a table, wait for the dealer to finish the hand in progress. Then you may buy chips by placing currency on the layout, pushing it toward the dealer, and saying, "Change, please."

Do not leave currency in the betting box on the table. In most of the newer gaming jurisdictions, casinos are not allowed to accept cash bets. However, casinos in some places allow cash bets with the call "Money plays." Don't leave the dealer wondering if that $100 bill is a request for change or a bet on the next hand. Once you make a bet, keep your hands off the chips in the betting box until the hand is over. If you are betting chips of different denominations, stack them with the smallest denomination on top. If you put a larger denomination on top, the dealer will rearrange them before going on with the hand. This is one way the casino guards against someone attempting to add a large-denomination chip to a bet after the outcome is known.

In multiple-deck games, give playing decisions with hand signals. In single- or double-deck games dealt facedown, pick up the cards with one hand, scratch the table with the cards for a hit, and slide the cards under your chips to stand. Turn the cards faceup if you bust or if you wish to split pairs or double down. At the conclusion of play, let the dealer turn any cards placed under your chips faceup.

If you wish to use the restroom and return to the same seat, you may ask the dealer to mark your place. A clear plastic disk will be placed in your betting box as a sign that the seat is occupied.

THE HOUSE EDGE

Because the player hands are completed first, the players have the chance to bust before the dealer plays. The house wins whenever the player busts, regardless of how the dealer's hand plays out. That is the entire source of the casino's advantage in Blackjack. Because of this one edge, the casino will win more hands than even the most expert player.

The casino gives back some of this advantage by paying 3–2 on Blackjack, allowing players to see one of the dealer's cards, and by letting the player double down and split pairs. To take advantage of these options, the player must learn proper strategy.

BASIC STRATEGY

Played well, Blackjack becomes a game of skill in a casino full of games of chance. Studies of millions of computer-generated hands have yielded a strategy for when to hit, when to stand, when to double down, and when to split. This strategy can bring the house edge down to about .5 percent in a six-deck game—and even lower in games with fewer decks. In a single-deck game in which the dealer stands on all 17s and the player is allowed to double down after splits, a basic strategy player can gain an edge of .1 percent over the house. (Needless to say, such single-deck games are not commonly dealt.)

Compare those percentages with players who adopt a never-bust strategy. This involves standing on all hands of 12 or more, so that drawing a 10-value card will not cause them to lose before the dealer's hand is played. Never-bust players and those who use dealer's strategy and always hit 16 or less and stand on 17 or more face a house edge estimated at 5 percent—about 10 times the edge faced by a basic strategy player.

Basic strategy takes advantage of the player's opportunity to look at one of the dealer's cards. In this case, you're not just blindly trying to come as close to 21 as possible. By showing you one card, the dealer allows you to make an educated estimate of the eventual outcome and play your cards accordingly.

One simple way to look at it is to play as if the dealer's facedown card is worth ten. Because 10-value cards (T, J, Q, K) comprise four of the 13 denominations in the deck, that is the single most likely value of any unseen card. Therefore, if you have 16 and the dealer's up card is a 7, you are guessing that the most likely dealer total is 17. The dealer would stand on 17 to beat your 16; therefore, you must hit the 16 to have the best chance to win. On the other hand, if you have 16 and the dealer's up card is a 6, your assumption would be that his total is 16, making the dealer more likely to bust on the next card. Therefore, you stand on 16 versus 6. That's an oversimplification, of course, but very close to the way the percentages work when the effect of multiple-card draws are taken into account.

The most common decision a player must make is whether to hit or stand on a hard total—a hand in which there is no ace being used as an 11. Basic strategy begins with the proper plays for each hard total. Many players seem to hit the wall at 16 and stand regardless of the dealer's up card. But that 16 is a loser unless the dealer busts, and the dealer will make 17 or better nearly 80 percent of the time with a 7 or higher showing. The risk of busting by hitting 16 is outweighed by the likelihood you'll lose if you stand.

Basic strategy for hard totals is straightforward enough, but when it comes to soft totals, many players become confused. Nothing you could draw can hurt a soft 16, or a soft 15, or many other soft totals. Just as with hard totals, guesswork is unnecessary. A basic strategy tells you what to do with soft hands. The hand of A-6 is the most misplayed hand in Blackjack. People who understand that the dealer always stands on 17 and that the player stands on hard 17 and above seem to think 17 is a good hand, but the dealer must bust for 17 to win. If the dealer does not bust, the best 17 can do is tie. By hitting soft 17, you have a chance to improve it by drawing A, 2, 3, or 4, or leave it the same with T, J, Q, or K. That's eight of 13 cards that either improve the hand or leave it no worse. And even if the draw is 5, 6, 7, 8, or 9, you have another chance to draw if the dealer shows 7 or better. And you're still in position to win if the dealer busts while showing 2 through 6, and all you've given up is a chance to tie a 17.

Standing on soft 18 will lose the player money in the long run when the dealer shows 9, T, or A. When the dealer shows 3 through 6, the chances of the dealer busting are strong enough to make doubling down the best play.

The final category of hands consists of those in which the first two cards match. Then the player must decide whether to split the pair into two hands. Basic strategy for pair splitting is included in the chart that follows. This basic strategy chart covers every hand in Blackjack. If you play with a strategy card, you will eventually memorize most of the correct plays and not need the card.

Be strategic and you can win when dealt these hands.

Your Hand	DEALER'S FACEUP CARD									
	2	3	4	5	6	7	8	9	10	A
HARD TOTALS (excluding pairs)										
17-20	S	S	S	S	S	S	S	S	S	S
16	S	S	S	S	S	H	H	H	H	H
15	S	S	S	S	S	H	H	H	H	H
13-14	S	S	S	S	S	H	H	H	H	H
12	H	H	S	S	S	H	H	H	H	H
11	DH	DH	DH	DH	DH	DH	DH	DH	DH	H
10	DH	DH	DH	DH	DH	DH	DH	DH	H	H
9	H	DH	DH	DH	DH	H	H	H	H	H
5-8	H	H	H	H	H	H	H	H	H	H
SOFT TOTALS										
A,8 A,9	S	S	S	S	S	S	S	S	S	S
A,7	S	DS	DS	DS	DS	S	S	H	H	H
A,6	H	DH	DH	DH	DH	H	H	H	H	H
A,4 A,5	H	H	DH	DH	DH	H	H	H	H	H
A,2 A,3	H	H	H	DH	DH	H	H	H	H	H
PAIRS										
A,A	SP	SP	SP	SP	SP	SP	SP	SP	SP	SP
10,10	S	S	S	S	S	S	S	S	S	S
9,9	SP	SP	SP	SP	SP	SP	SP	SP	S	S
8,8	SP	SP	SP	SP	SP	SP	SP	SP	SP	SP
7,7	SP	SP	SP	SP	SP	SP	H	H	H	H
6,6	SP	SP	SP	SP	SP	H	H	H	H	H
5,5	DH	DH	DH	DH	DH	DH	DH	DH	H	H
4,4	H	H	H	SP	SP	H	H	H	H	H
2,2 3,3	SP	SP	SP	SP	SP	SP	H	H	H	H

*Key: S=Stand, H=Hit, DH=Double down (hit when not allowed),
DS=Double down (stand when not allowed), SP=Split*

CONTRACT BRIDGE

Contract Bridge took off as an international rage in the 1930s and is considered by many to be the ultimate card game. Even those who have been playing for decades still find room to learn.

♣ ♦ ♠ ♥

PLAYERS

Four, playing as two pairs, with partners facing each other. Tradition refers to the pairs as North-South and East-West.

OBJECT

Following an auction, to score points by taking tricks during the play and to eventually win a rubber of two games.

CARDS

Each deal requires a regular pack of 52 cards. It's customary to keep a second pack ready for the next hand.

PLAYING

After all the cards have been dealt out, dealer begins the auction (also called the bidding). Don't let any other player see your cards during the auction. When the bidding is over, the play of the hand starts. The play comprises 13 tricks in all.

UNDERSTANDING THE BIDDING

Most games with auctions or bids use a brief and simple procedure. Bridge is special in allowing players to have a creative and complex auction.

In Bridge, players on both sides bid for their side's right to choose the trump suit or to play the hand at NT (no-trump). The dealer starts the bidding. A bid is a number 1-7 plus a suit (♣, ♦, ♥, ♠, or NT). The number, added to six, indicate how many tricks your side is to take with the suit bid as trumps.

Each time it's your turn, you may bid or pass (make no bid). Simply put, if you can manage to win the bid at a suit in which your side has more cards than the other side has, it will greatly help in winning tricks.

The lowest bid, 1♣, is a contract your side would fulfill by taking at least 7 tricks with clubs as trumps. Similarly, 1♦ indicates 7 tricks with diamonds as trumps; 3♦ means 9 tricks with diamonds as trumps; 3 NT means 9 tricks with no suit as trumps.

The bidding can start with any opening bid. During the auction, players in turn may pass or bid (or in frequent cases, may double or redouble). Each new bid must be higher than the previous bid. The new bid may be in a higher-ranking suit without increasing the number of tricks: ♣s rank lowest, followed by ♦, ♥, ♠, and NT. (In Bridge, ♥s and ♠s are called majors; ♣s and ♦s are called minors). Or, if you go to a higher number of tricks, you can bid in any suit or NT.

The auction ends as soon as three players in a row pass. The last bid becomes the final contract. The last bidder is called the declarer. The declarer's partner has the dummy hand.

DOUBLE AND REDOUBLE

If your opponent has made the most recent bid, at your turn you may double (just say the word "double"). This means you double the stakes, i.e., if you make your contract, you win double the number of points—your risk is also correspondingly greater. Either opponent can then redouble. Three passes end every auction, so it's quite possible for the final contract to be doubled or redoubled, increasing the score.

THE PLAY OF THE HAND

Let's look at a sample bid and how it then plays out.

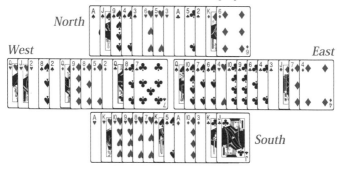

In the diagrammed deal, West deals and passes, and North opens the bidding 1♠. East passes. South bids 2♥. West passes. North bids 3♥ and, after East passes, South bids 6♥. This is a bid to take 12 out of the 13 tricks on the hand, which South expects to happen. The next three players all pass. South, the first to bid ♥s for the winning bidders, becomes declarer at a contract of 6♥.

West, the player at declarer's left, will choose the card to lead to the first trick. This is called the opening lead. Once the opening lead is made, the dummy hand, (that of declarer's partner, here North), is placed on the table. North rearranges it to show trumps on the left:

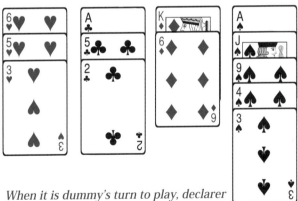

When it is dummy's turn to play, declarer selects the card to be played and plays it or asks dummy to play what the declarer selects. Each hand in playing to a trick must follow with a card of the suit led, but lacking that suit may play any card. Whichever hand wins a trick will lead any card to the next trick.

West begins by lending the ♦5. Playing low from dummy, South wins East's ♦J with the ♦A. At tricks two and three, South cashes (takes short tricks) his ♥A and ♥K, and discovers that the defense will win a trick with the ♥Q. That's okay, as South will win every other trick. South continues at the fourth trick by leading the ♦3 to dummy's ♦K, and then comes back to hand by leading ♠3 to the ♠K. South next leads the ♦10, West puts on the ♦Q, but South trumps it in dummy with dummy's remaining trump. Except for West's high♥, South will win all the tricks and the contract succeeds.

SCORING

After the tricks have been played, it is clear whether the declarer made the contract (i.e., took at least the number of tricks bid for) or, instead, went down. If the contract is made, the declaring side scores according to the table on page 33. If you make a contract of 6, it's called a small slam; a grand slam is a made contract of 7 bids. Both slams receive bonuses. If you win six or seven tricks but did not bid that number, you are not credited with a slam.

If the contract goes down, the other side scores points for under-tricks, that is, the number of tricks the declaring side falls short of the contract (see the table).

RUBBER BRIDGE SCORING

When one side has scored two games, it wins the rubber. A game means 100 points in tricks bid for (and won) according to the scoring table. It's quite possible to bid and make game on a single deal: For example, 3 NT scores 100 points. Alternatively, you can earn game in a series of deals whose final contracts end at a lower bidding level; these are called part-scores or partials. For example, you might bid and make 2♦ on one hand (40 points), and on the next hand you might bid and make 2♥ (60 points). The two added together equal 100 points, enough for game.

A side that has scored one game is vulnerable, so if both sides have a game both are vulnerable. A side that hasn't scored a game yet is not vulnerable. When defenders defeat, or set, a contract, they earn greater points whenever the other side is vulnerable. Score for the winning side is also increased when the final contract is doubled or redoubled. Note: Extra tricks (overtricks) made at any contract do not count toward game.

SCORING ABOVE AND BELOW THE LINE

Both sides usually keep score, either on a preprinted Bridge score pad, or else just by drawing lines in a cross. Points toward game go below the line, while all other points, including bonuses and overtricks, score above the line.

TIPS AND STRATEGY

Remembering the cards played is one key to improving your play. This will occur over time. As a start, make sure to notice and remember the first time someone doesn't follow to a trick. It also helps to develop an ease with the number 13! That's the number of cards in a suit, the number or cards each player is dealt, and the number of tricks in the play.

BRIDGE SCORING

Contract level	minors (♣/♦)	majors(♥/♠)	NT
1	20	30	40
2	40	60	70
3	60	90	100
4	80	120	130
5	100	150	160
6	120	180	190
7	140	210	220

SCORING FOR UNDERTRICKS

"Down" means number of tricks short of the contract.

		Not vulnerable Doubled	Redoubled		Vulnerable Doubled	Redoubled
Down 1	50	100	200	100	200	400
Down 2	100	300	600	200	500	1000
Down 3	150	500	1000	300	800	1600
Down 4	200	800	1600	400	1100	2200
Down 5	250	1100	2200	500	1400	2800
Down 6	300	1400	2800	600	1700	3400

SCORING FOR BONUSES

Rubber bonus	500 (2 games to 1), or 700 (2 games to 0)
Small slam	500 not vulnerable, 750 vulnerable

Grand slam	1,000 not vulnerable, 1,500 vulnerable
Bonus for making doubled contract	50
Bonus for making redoubled contract	100
Honors: All four aces in one hand, at a NT contract	150
Honors: Top 5 trumps all in one hand	150
Honors: 4 of 5 top trumps all in one hand	100
Overtricks: Undoubled (each)	Clubs or diamonds, 20; Hearts, aces, or NT, 30
Overtricks: Doubled (each)	not vulnerable, 100, vulnerable 200
Overtricks: Redoubled (each)	not vulnerable, 200, vulnerable 400

Auction: bidding for number of tricks to be taken in the game

Contract: number of tricks declarer must take to satisfy his or her bid

Declarer: winner of the auction, the player who tries to make the contract

Dummy: declarer's partner; the dummy hand is laid face up on the table

Double: in the auction a bid to double the score or the penalties if a contract is made or set

Major: a heart or spade card

Minor: a diamond or club card

Not vulnerable: a side that has not won a game yet in a rubber.

Redouble: doubling a double

Response: your call in the auction when your partner has opened the bidding

Raise: a bid in a suit that partner has already bid

Rebid: your second bid

Overcall: a bid made after opponents have opened the bidding

Set: to defeat a contract

Undertricks: number of tricks the declaring side falls short of the contract

Table: the dummy

Rubber: two games

Ruff: to trump

Singleton: just one card of a suit

Void: no cards in a suit

Vulnerable: a side that has won a game in a rubber

HONEYMOON BRIDGE

This is one of the most popular two-player Bridge variants.

♣ ♦ ♠ ♥

PLAYERS

Two

OBJECT

This is a great game for couples. Players sit next to (not opposite) each other. Dealer deals out four hands, including a dummy hand for each player. Deal each dummy hand as follows: First, deal out two rows of three cards face down. Then place one card face up on top of each face-down card. Deal the last card face up next to the rows.

Bid as in normal Bridge, except that a single pass ends the auction. The play goes this way, with each player controlling the cards played from the partner/dummy hand across the table: The hand at declarer's left makes the opening lead. Players select the cards played only from among the exposed cards in their dummy hands. After the trick is finished, turn up any uncovered card in their dummy. Any newly revealed card may now be played.

CUTTHROAT BRIDGE

Cutthroat Bridge (also called Three-Handed Bridge) is a three-player game.

♣ ♦ ♠ ♥

PLAYING

As in Contract Bridge, players draw for deal but do not draw for partners. The dealer then deals out four hands. The fourth hand becomes the dummy and is left facedown during the bidding, which is the same as Contract Bridge except that a bid stands after two consecutive passes instead of three. The dummy hand is then revealed and placed across from the declarer between the two other players after the player to the left of him/her leads. The two opponents become partners for that hand.

Ensuing hands may create different partnerships. The score sheet is divided into three columns, one for each player. If the declarer fills his/her contract, the declarer scores the points for the hand under normal Contract Bridge rules. If the declarer does not fulfill the contract, opponents are awarded the set points. The rubber ends when any one of the three players has won two games.

When playing Cutthroat Bridge, the strategy is slightly different because there is no way of gaining additional information about the dummy hand until after the bidding process.

REVERSE BRIDGE

This four-handed game turns all the rules upside-down!

♣ ♦ ♠ ♥

PLAYING

Rules and play are as in standard Contract Bridge, but the object is entirely the opposite: You try to force opponents to take the tricks for the bid you make. So, if your side wins a final contract of 4♠, your job is to get your opponents to take at least 10 of 13 tricks with ♠ as trumps. You get the score for any contract you force the opponents to make!

STRATEGY

Instead of saving the high cards your side holds to play on different tricks, as in regular Bridge, you'll play as high a card as you can that you think will still lose a trick. When your side does take a trick, try to put high cards on it from both hands so that you can save your losing cards to help you later in the hand!

AUCTION BRIDGE

Auction Bridge had its heyday from about 1900 to
1930, before yielding to Contract Bridge.

♣ ♦ ♠ ♥

PLAYERS

Four

OBJECT

To score points. In Auction Bridge, if you take enough tricks, you
score game and slam bonuses without regard to how high the
bidding ended.

CARDS

Regular pack of 52.

PLAYING

The auction, procedure of play, and rules of play are the same as
in Contract Bridge.

SCORING

Auction Bridge underwent several scoring changes, and this is the final version. A rubber ends when one side scores two games. Game is 30 points in trick-score: ♣, ♦, ♥, ♠, and NT score 6, 7, 8, 9, and 10 points per trick, scored below the line. When one side reaches 30, both sides start anew on the next game. Winning the rubber (two games) earns a 250-point bonus.

Winning 12 of 13 tricks earns a 50-point small slam bonus, and winning all 13 tricks (a grand slam) receives a 100-point reward. Making doubled or redoubled contracts doubles or redoubles the trick-score. Overtricks (extra tricks made) at a doubled contract count 50 each, and redoubled overtricks are 100 each. Failing to make a contract costs 50 per trick undoubled, 100 doubled, and 200 redoubled.

Bonuses are given to hands that contain any of the following:

3 of top 5 honors (A, K, Q, J, and 10 of trump) or 3 aces at NT (may be divided between hands)	30 points;
4 honors or 4 aces at NT (divided)	40 points
5 trump honors divided	50 points
4 trump honors in one hand	80 points;
4 trump honors in one hand, with 5th in partner's hand	100 points
4 aces in one hand (at NT)	100 points
5 honors in one hand	150 points

TIPS

Look to take as many tricks as you can, since the possibility of winning a game or slam is alive on every hand.

CANASTA

This high-scoring card game is a great choice for at-home parties. It's both strategic and fun to play. Canasta means "basket" in Spanish, and it probably refers to the tray that held the discards. Canasta originated in Uruguay in the early 1940s and became widely popular in North America in the 1950s.

♣ ♦ ♠ ♥

PLAYERS

Four, in partnerships seated across the table

OBJECT

To score points by melding, with the goal of scoring a canasta and then going out.

CARDS

Two regular packs of 52 cards plus their four jokers are used. Jokers and deuces are wild.

MELDING

Melds must consist of at least three cards, all of the same rank. All melds are placed face up on the table, and partners build up their melds together to form canastas, seven-card bonus melds.

All jokers and deuces are wild and can be used in melds as any desired rank except 3s. A canasta must consist of at least four natural cards but may contain any number of wild cards.

THE TREYS

Red 3s are bonus cards worth 100 points each, but they are not used in play. You should lay down a red 3 as soon as you can. If your side scores all four red 3s, the bonus for them doubles to 800 points.

Black 3s are used in play, but are meldable only when going out. Otherwise, they function as stopper cards (see "Freezing the Pack" on page 44).

PLAYING

Deal 11 cards to each player, one at a time, then turning over an upcard that starts a discard pile called the pack. The remainder of the cards form the stock. Note: If the upcard is a wild card or a red 3, turn another card up on top of it, and see "Freezing the pack."

The player at dealer's left goes first, with play passing in clockwise rotation until the hand is over. At your turn, even on the first round of play, you may take the pack with an appropriate hand of cards (see "Taking the Pack"), but your usual turn consists of drawing one card and then discarding one card on top of the pack.

INITIAL MELDS

The first player to meld for a side must table at least 50 points of meld. All cards have point values for melding.

To calculate the value of a meld, simply add up the value of the cards it contains. Note that a three-card (or longer)

Joker	50 points
Deuce	20 points
Ace	20 points
King through 8	10 points
7 through 4	5 points
Black 3s	5 points

meld must have at least two natural cards. The initial melding requirement increases along the way as detailed in the table below:

Score at the beginning of new deal	Minimum initial meld
Less than 0	15 points
0–1495	50 points
1500–2995	90 points
3000 or more	120 points

TAKING THE PACK

You are allowed to take the pack—the entire current pile of discards—as long as you can meld the top discard and meet the following conditions. If your side hasn't melded yet, you'll need two natural (not wild) cards to meld with the upcard, and you must meet the minimum meld required for your side (without using any other cards in the pack). If your side has melded already, then one natural card with one wild card will do, and you may even take the pack if your opponent's discard can go into one of your melds.

Also, once your side has met its initial meld, you may use the pack to form new melds or add to your melds to form canastas, as you wish. Any cards you don't meld become part of your hand.

Once a meld is on the table, either partner may play off it. When a meld contains seven or more cards, it becomes a canasta. It is squared into a pile and a red card is placed on top if it consists of all natural cards (a natural canasta). A black card is placed on top if it contains any wild cards (a mixed canasta). If any wild cards are later added to a red canasta, it becomes a black canasta, and its value changes accordingly.

You don't have to take the pack to make an initial meld, but it gives you more cards to play with. Wait until there are enough cards (around 10 to 12) in the pack to take it, so you will have more cards in your hand. In this case, taking the upcard gives you melds worth 90 points: ♦Q-♣Q-♠Q and ♥7-♥7-joker.

FREEZING THE PACK

Freezing the pack makes it difficult for any player to take the pack. To freeze the pack, discard a wild card sideways across the discards. The next player can't take the pack as long as the wild card remains. To pick up a frozen pack, you'll need a natural pair in your hand to go with top discard. This rule applies to all players, regardless of who froze the pack initially.

A black 3 freezes the pack momentarily, except in the unlikely event that a player with two black 3s can go out while taking the pack. That would require using every card taken in the pack. (Note: Wild cards may not meld with black 3s.) When a player discards one card face up on the pack, the turn is complete.

GOING OUT

You go out (sometimes called going rummy) if you meld all the cards in your hand. However, in order to go out, your side has to have at least one canasta, and in most games you need one card left over to discard. Play ceases at this point, and the score for the hand is tallied. Before going out, you are allowed to ask your partner "May I go out?" but you must abide by the answer.

Should no one go rummy, the hand ends when the stock is gone and the pack can't be taken.

SCORING

Total the value of all melded cards and add bonuses for going rummy (100), natural canastas (500), mixed canastas (300), and red 3s (100 each, but 800 for all four). Subtract the total of cards left in each player's hand (red 3s count –200 points), and tally each team's score. Game is 5,000 points.

TIP

When taking the pack, don't meld everything in it immediately. It is wise to keep some cards so that you'll have natural pairs to take a frozen pack.

CASINO

As far back as 1797, Casino was described in books on card games. Though the game has quite a few details, it's easy to learn and fun to play, with lots of suspense and surprise.

♣ ♦ ♠ ♥

PLAYERS

Two

OBJECT

To score points by taking cards.

CARDS

A regular pack of 52 cards is used.

PLAYING

Deal four cards to each player and four cards face up on the table. Dealer keeps the rest of the pack handy. Nondealer plays a card first; players then alternate until the round is over. You can combine the card you play with cards on the table in many possible ways.

MATCHING

If your card matches by rank a card on the table, you can take the pair immediately. Place the two cards face down in front of you. Face cards can be taken only with other face cards and only in pairs—if two queens are on the table and you hold another queen, you can take only one of the queens. However, if three matching face cards are on the table and you hold the fourth, you can take all four.

COMBINING

If your card equals the combined sum of two or more cards on the table, you can take those cards immediately.

BUILDING

If at least one free card on the table plus the card you play totals the number of a card in your hand, announce this build number and pile up the build to take later. For example, if there is a 6 on the table and you have a 3 and a 9 in your hand, you could play the 3 onto the 6 and say "Building 9s." On your next turn, if opponent hasn't taken it, you can take the build with your 9.

Opponent can change the value of a build by playing another card. In this case, opponent can play an ace on the build and say "Building 10s." This tells you he or she has a 10 with which to take the build. But if your 9-build is still there and if you have two 9s in your hand, on your next turn you can put one of them on top of the build and say "Still building 9s," intending to take the build with your remaining 9. This creates a double build. Players can't change the value of a double build.

Once you have made a build, on your next turn you must either take the build, add to the build, or make a new build. Leaving a build untaken runs the risk that opponent will take it, but you may leave a build behind as long as you can add cards to it or make another play.

Nothing prevents you from taking opponent's build; you can do so if you have the right card. On the other hand, nothing prevents your opponent from taking your build!

With this Casino hand, you can take the ♦9 with your ♥9 and take the ♥5 and ♠5 with your ♠10.

TRAILING

You may also play a card by trailing it—placing it on the table without building it onto another card. You can't do this if you have made a build that's still on the table. You must trail a card if you can't do anything else on your turn. For strategic reasons, a player might want to trail a card onto the table even though it matches the rank of one already there.

After the first round of four cards, dealer deals another round of four cards each and nondealer again plays first. Continue dealing four-card rounds until the pack is depleted, with dealer announcing "last" on the last round. Whoever makes the last take of the last round gets any cards left on the table.

Play to 21 points or to any other agreed number.

SCORING

Players count their cards and note the cards with extra value. Each deal contains 11 points:

◆10 (Big Casino)	2 points
♠2 (Little Casino)	1 point
♠A, ♣A, ♥A, ◆ A	1 point each
Majority of spades (7 or more)	1 point
Majority of cards (27 or more)	3 points (If tied at 26 cards, neither player wins these points.)

TIPS

Keeping track of what's been played—particularly the spades and points you've taken in—is critical in Casino.

Until it's been played, a certain amount of tension revolves around the ◆ 10, Big Casino. As nondealer, if you have the ◆ 10, you risk losing it if you can't take it in. (Dealer will probably save any 10 as the final card of the round.) Beware of building 10s when your own 10 is not the ◆ 10.

If you are dealt any of the four aces or the ♠2, your best chance of taking them in is through building. Test your opponent's hand with a double build. Suppose you're holding an ace, a 3, and a 6, and on the table are a 3 and a 5. You'd really like to take the ace for the point. First you play the 3 on the 3, saying "Building 6s." If opponent doesn't take it, on your next play you place your ace on the 5 to make a double build of 6s—subsequently picking up the lot with your 6.

You can often rack up more points by concentrating on winning cards and spades rather than on the Big Casino and Little Casino.

As dealer, if you are dealt a face card on the last round, you are virtually guaranteed to get last card, since you play last.

ROYAL CASINO

Here's a new twist on Casino that adds further strategy to a great old game.

♣ ♦ ♠ ♥

PLAYING

Play as regular Casino, with face cards having extra numerical values: Jacks are 11, queens 12, kings 13, aces 1 or 14. A queen, for example, can take an 8 and a 4. Aces on the table count 1, but an ace you play counts as 1 or 14, as you wish. So, an ace and a king on the table can be captured with an ace from your hand, since 1 + 13 = 14.

TIPS

In Royal Casino it's tempting to hold on to aces longer, because there's the chance to make or build 14. Just when you decide to play an ace will vary, depending on the cards already played and the other cards in your hand.

Picture cards no longer are taken only in pairs. So, dealer's "automatic" capture of last cards in regular Casino when dealer has at least one face card disappears. A face card at the end of a Royal Casino hand may indeed be an odd card. Or, even when opponent and you each hold a jack, for example, opponent can use it as an 11 and remove it from play.

CRAZY EIGHTS

Eights are wild and so is the action in this fast-paced game
that's easy to learn and perfect for families or parties.

♣ ♦ ♠ ♥

PLAYERS

Two to six. (Even more can play, but with more players, each
person has to wait longer between turns.)

OBJECT

To be the first player to get rid of all your cards.

CARDS

A regular pack of 52 cards. With four or more players you might
want to use two packs.

PLAYING

Deal seven cards each, turn one card up to start a discard pile,
and leave the remainder of the cards next to the pile as a draw
stack. The player at the dealer's left begins by covering the

upcard with a matching card—either the same suit or same rank. For example, if the starter card is ♦7, you can play any diamond or 7. When you can't match, draw cards from stock until you can.

All 8s are wild and can be played at any time. Call the 8 any suit for the next player to match. Don't specify rank. Don't get caught holding 8s at the end of play, since they count for a whopping 50 points each!

Play rotates to the left, as each player matches the top card, and continues until one player has no cards left. If you run out of draw cards, simply turn the discard pile facedown, shuffle, and use it for a new draw pile.

To match the ♣4, choose ♥4, ♣K, or ♣7. Save the wild card (♥8) for when you really need it!

SCORING

Whoever goes out scores the point total of cards left in everyone else's hands. Each 8 is worth 50, face cards are worth 10, and all others are face value (ace = 1). The game usually ends after an agreed time limit or number of deals.

TIPS

When you have many cards of one suit, others may find that suit hard to match. Remember, in a game with several players, your play affects the next player most.

VARIATIONS

In Double Crazy Eights, turn the upcard sideways so that two piles can fit on it. As play goes on, you may choose which pile to play on. You may still play an 8 at anytime, but you must match it next by its original suit.

In Double Crazy Eights you have one more element to consider in playing. Example: You think your opponent has no diamonds and one of the piles has a diamond on top. If you can place a diamond on top of the other pile, you might force your opponent to draw cards.

CRIBBAGE

Cribbage is thought to have been invented in the
17th century by Sir John Suckling. It was the favorite
card game of Mr. and Mrs. Benjamin Franklin.

♣ ♦ ♠ ♥

PLAYERS

Two

OBJECT

To score points by forming certain card combinations and to be
first to reach 121 (or 61) points.

CARDS

A regular pack of 52 cards is used. Each card has a point value
equal to its rank. Aces are low and count 1. Face cards count 10.

SCORING COMBINATIONS

Fifteen: any combination of cards totaling exactly 15 points	2 points
Pair: two cards of the same rank	2 points
Triplet: three cards of the same rank	6 points
Quartet: four cards of the same rank	12 points
Sequence: three or more cards in a row, any suit (aces always low)	1 point per card
Flush: four cards of the same suit	1 point per card
Jack of the start card's suit	1 point

THE CRIBBAGE BOARD

The board has 30 holes in each of four rows, marked off in groups of five. Each player gets two pegs. In the beginning the four pegs sit at the start end of the board. The pegs move up the outside row and down the inside row back to the start, for a total of 61 points. The usual game is two trips, or 121 points. The two pegs are used alternately, the back peg leapfrogging over the front peg. If you do not have a Cribbage board, you can use paper and pencil to keep score.

PLAYING

Deal six cards each, one at a time. Both players select two cards to discard together. These cards are put face down to form a four-card crib belonging to the dealer.

Next, nondealer cuts the pack and dealer turns up the top card. This is the start card. If the start card is a jack, dealer pegs 2 (scores 2 points).

Nondealer now plays any one card from hand face up, calling out its value. Dealer does the same, calling out the total of the two cards played. The two players continue back and forth in this way without exceeding 31. If you cannot play without going past 31, say "Go," which instructs your opponent to continue playing as many cards as possible without going past 31. Opponent pegs 1 for your go if able to play under 31. A player who reaches 31 exactly pegs 2 points. One more point is pegged by whoever plays the last card. When both players are unable to play, a new count is started by the player who did not make the most recent play.

PEGGING FOR MELDS

In addition to the scoring for go, 31, and last card, combinations made during play score points. If your play makes the count 15, score 2. If you match the rank of the card played by opponent, score 2 for the pair. Three cards of the same rank are worth 6 points, and the fourth one scores 12. Sequences also count, and the cards don't have to be in exact order. For example, 3-6-4-5 scores 4 points for the last player, and if the next player follows with a deuce, that sequence is worth 5 points. A flush (series of cards of the same suit) does not score in play; it scores only when scoring the hand. Cards must be played consecutively within one 31-count to score.

The play of the cards can take different paths. Nondealer might start with the ♦2. Dealer plays ♠2, saying, "Four for two," and pegging two for the pair. Nondealer plays ♦K, bringing the count to 14. Dealer can now play the ♥A and reach 15 for 2 points, but the better play is the ♥K, saying, "24 for two," (another pair). Nondealer plays the ♥4, for 28, and dealer plays ♠3 bringing the count to exactly 31, which scores another 2. Nondealer then starts the count again with the ♣A, saying, "One," and dealer plays the ♥A, saying "Two for two (another pair!), and one for last card." Dealer has pegged 9 points in play!

SCORING THE HANDS

After the cards have been played out, each player's hand and dealer's crib are counted and scored. Nondealer's hand pegs first, then dealer's. The start card is scored as a fifth card in each hand.

By custom, nondealer now gathers up all the cards except the crib and the start. Dealer then turns up the crib and pegs its score. With a crib of 10-3-7-8 and a start card of 9, dealer would say, "15-2 and a four-card run makes 6."

Because Cribbage scoring is involved and precise, many players follow the rule of Muggins. In this variation, players count aloud their points and the crib. If any points are overlooked, the opponent says aloud "Muggins" and takes the points overlooked into their own tally.

PEGGING OUT

As soon as one player pegs to 121 (or 61, in a shorter game), the game ends. If you win by more than 60 points (a skunk), score for a double game.

TIPS

One of the fine arts of Cribbage is choosing which cards to go into the crib and which cards to keep. If you have a high-scoring four-card group, such as 7-8-8-9, keep them and put the other two in the crib.

If it's your own crib, put scoring cards such as pairs and 15s (or at least a 5-spot) into the crib, when this also leaves you a reasonable hand. In general, put middle-range cards (4 through 8) in your own crib, and put high and low cards (2s and kings) in your opponent's. Take into account how many start cards will be good for the various choices of cards to keep. Likewise, consider how different start cards can combine with your crib discards.

The cards you choose for the crib depend a lot on whose crib it is. If it's opponent's crib (left), keep both fives and put the 10 and 3 in the crib (or the 10 and the 8). If it's your crib, you are happy to put the 8-7 "15 combination" in the crib, keeping the 10 in your hand with both fives.

In play, start with a card that counts under 5 so that opponent can't peg an immediate 15.

Near the end of the game, scoring order can greatly influence your discards and your decisions in play. For example, if you need just 3 or 4 points to win, then you don't need a high-scoring hand.

Try to keep cards that will permit you to win during the play-out.

Similarly, when dealer is 5 or 10 points from winning, opponent needs to score points soon and may have to gamble on getting help from the start card for a high-scoring hand.

DUROCK

This popular Russian game of attack and defense uses trumps in a most unusual way. Durock, incidentally, means "fool!"

♣ ♦ ♠ ♥

PLAYERS

Two or more, but this is an especially good game for five players.

OBJECT

Not to be Durock, the last player left with cards.

CARDS

One regular pack of 52.

PLAYING

Deal five cards to each player. Turn up the next card, which designates the trump suit. Leave it visible but under the rest of the undealt cards, the stock (or talon). Aces are high.

Play consists of a clockwise progression of attack and defense. Attacker plays one to five cards on the table. The next player defends the attack with two options: Either pick up and keep the attacking cards, or else beat each attack card.

THE ATTACK

The attack may be any of these plays: a single card, a pair (two cards of the same rank), three of a kind (three cards of the same rank), two pairs, four of a kind (four cards of the same suit), or a full house (a pair plus 3 of a kind).

To defend, you must beat each card in the attack by a higher card in the same suit or by a trump card.

In the hand shown, ♦s are trump and Eddie has attacked Jill with ♣4 ♥4 ♠9 ♣9. Jill could have picked up these cards,    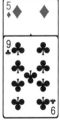 *but her hand happens to be good enough to beat each: She plays ♣J ♥8 ♠A ♦5, topping each attack card with a higher card in that suit or with a trump.*

JOINING THE ATTACK

Other players may add, at any time, more cards of the same rank as an attack card. At no time may the total number of attack cards be larger than 5, however. In the example hand, any other player could add to the attack with a 4 or a 9. Since the attack must stop with 5 cards, this time only one player can add to the attack. For example, if Victor adds the ♦9, Jill will have to top it with a higher trump, or else pick up all the cards.

Note that attack cards up to a limit of five can still be thrown even as defender is picking up the earlier part of the attack.

If the defender beats every attack card, then all cards involved are retired from play.

REPLENISHING HANDS

Starting with attacker and including defender, all players with zero to four cards now draw from the talon until each has five cards again. Any player with 5 or more cards does not draw.

ONGOING PLAY

If successful, the defender now becomes the new attacker. If the defender picked up cards, then the following player makes the next clockwise attack.

Play continues like this until the talon is exhausted. (The trump upcard is the last card drawn.) Here's when the fun really begins! Now, as soon as you have no cards left, you're out of the hand and you can't be Durock; you can relax and watch the others play.

When only two players remain, if one attacks using all their remaining cards, the other player is Durock without getting a chance to defend.

By tradition, Durock takes on the shame of gathering, shuffling, cutting, and dealing the cards for the next hand. Also by tradition, if someone other than Durock touches the cards, that person becomes dealer!

NOTE

At the end of the hand, a player with fewer than five cards can be attacked only up to the number of cards held. Example: Victor has 3 cards. Hugo attacks him with 2 cards, as Jill adds a third. Eddie cannot join the attack. Victor picks up those cards, and now that he has 6 cards, he may receive a full attack the next time.

SCORING

If you are playing for a stake, Durock pays one chip to each other player.

TIPS

It does not hurt to pick up attack cards in the early stages. You'll still have chances to get rid of many of these cards before players start to drop out. In fact you can gather high cards of the same rank, such as three kings, and use them to counter an attack. If you have trumps, especially high ones, they will be most helpful in the endgame. Also, when your right-hand opponent is defender, by withholding from the attack, or by adding to it, you may influence whether he or she succeeds or fails.

VARIATIONS

In a large game, the right to join the attack may be limited to the players nearest the attacker.

Pass-the-Buck : Under this rule, the defender who can match the attack card passes the attack along onto the next player, who takes over as defender. Example: Meg is attacked with ♠6. Meg plays ♣6 and passes the pair of 6s along to the next player, Stan, who becomes the defender.

A popular traditional Durock variant limits the initial attack to one rank, but any new card defender plays opens up that rank for attack too. Example: ♦s are trump. Hugo plays ♥5 at Victor. Victor plays ♥7 to beat the attack, but then Hugo extends the attack by playing the ♣7, while Eddie tosses on the ♠7! Victor may want to pick up the pile now, before it gets any bigger!

Durock with six cards dealt is a popular form of the game. Also, some prefer to play with a 36-card pack created by removing all 2s through 5s.

ELEUSIS

Over four decades ago, Robert Abbott developed this unusual card game. Nowadays, other versions exist, but this one, close to the original, is one of the most inviting.

♣ ♦ ♠ ♥

PLAYERS

At least three

OBJECT

To get rid of as many cards as you can by discovering the rule of play governing the hand.

CARDS

A regular pack of 52 cards.

PLAYING

Dealer turns the top card up as a starter, then deals the whole pack out to the other players—dealer gets no cards. Dealer now writes down a secret rule of play, simple or complicated, guiding the cards players may legally discard from their hand onto the starter pile. Dealer puts the secret rule out of sight until the end of the hand.

At your turn, you must play at least one card on the discard pile. Dealer says, "Right," if your play follows the rule. Then the next player goes. However, if your play is illegal, dealer says, "Wrong," and you must leave any cards played face up in front of you, where they still count as part of your hand. You may try playing these exposed cards later. If your play contains a series of cards, each one in turn must be a correct play.

In the example shown, with the start card the ♦ 10, dealer's rule was if the card is even and red, play a heart; if the card is even and black, play a diamond; if the card is odd and red, play a spade; and if the card is odd and black, play a club (jack and king are considered odd, queen is even). All cards added on must comply with the rule, though players may still not have figured out why!

Game is over when one player has no cards, either in hand or on the table. Game also may end when dealer affirms that no player has a legal play and the game is blocked (dealer may show the written rule at this point). The winner is the first to play out all his or her cards, or, in a blocked game, the one with the fewest cards left. Deal rotates to the left for each new hand.

SCORING

Losers double the difference between the number of cards they
hold and the number the winner has left (if any). Winner and
dealer split these winnings equally. Example: In a four-player
game, the winner has two cards left while first loser has three
and second loser has nine. First loser scores –2, second loser
scores –14, and winner and dealer each score +8.

In case two players tie for the fewest cards, dealer still receives
half the losing sums, while the winners share what's left. Since
dealer always wins, be sure everybody gets an equal number of
deals.

TIPS

Since as dealer you get your best score when one player figures
out the rule and can get way ahead of the other players, use your
judgment of the other players to design a rule one of them may
figure out more quickly than the others.

Here are two examples of rules you can use: (1) If the card is a
diamond, play any other suit; if the card is a club, play a red card;
if the card is a spade, play a black card; if the card is a heart,
play a card of the same rank. (2) If the sum of the last two cards
played is 2–8, play a spade; if the sum of the cards is 9–12 play
a club; if the sum is 13–16 play a diamond; if the sum is 17 or
more, play a heart (picture cards count 10, Ace = 1).

EUCHRE

Euchre is thought to have descended from a popular sixteenth-century game. A hundred years ago in America, it had plenty of devotees and was considered our national game!

♣ ♦ ♠ ♥

PLAYERS

Four, with partners seated facing each other. Euchre may also be played by two or three players.

OBJECT

To score points by winning at least three of five tricks.

CARDS

A 32-card pack, 7s through aces for each suit, is used. All 2s through 6s are discarded before play. Cards rank as follows: A-K-Q-J-10-9-8-7, except in trumps, where the jack (called the right bower) is high, and the other jack of the same color (the left bower) is the second highest trump.

Special Euchre decks are also available. Euchre can also be played with 24 cards (7s and 8s omitted) or 28 cards (7s omitted).

DEALING

Players draw cards to set pairs and decide the dealer. Only in determining partners is the ace considered low. Those who draw the two highest cards play against the other two players. Lowest card deals first. Those who draw the same rank, draw again. Henceforth, the deal rotates clockwise. Five cards are dealt to each player either in batches of two and three or three and two. After the hands are dealt, the dealer turns up the top card from the stock to begin the task of setting trump. By custom, it stays on the table, while the card it replaces is put beneath the remaining undealt cards.

THE TRUMP SUIT

Starting at dealer's left, each player has a chance to accept or pass the suit turned as trumps. To accept, an opponent of the dealer says "I order it up," dealer's partner says "I assist," and dealer accepts by discarding. Any player may pass.

On balance, to accept you should judge your side at least a two-to-one favorite, since you win only one point when you succeed (unless you score a march), but lose two points when you fail (see "Scoring"). If all four players pass, dealer places the upcard under the pack of undealt cards, and another round follows to find a trump suit. Starting with the player at dealer's left, each may pass until one player names a trump suit other than the suit first turned up. If all players again pass, throw the cards in and shuffle for a new deal.

When accepting or naming a trump suit, you may also declare at that time to play alone. Your partner's hand is put aside, and you play against both opponents.

The player at dealer's left usually leads to the first trick, but when you play a lone hand, the defender at your right leads first.

On each trick, follow to the suit of the card led if possible. Otherwise, play any card. Each trick is won by the highest card of the suit led, except a trick containing at least one trump, which is won by the highest trump played. Note that the ♥J is not considered a heart when diamonds are trumps!

SCORING

The game is played to a predetermined number of points, usually 5, 7, or 10.

Declaring side wins three or four tricks	1 point
Declaring side wins five tricks (a march)	4 points
If lone hand wins	4 points
Declaring side euchred (wins fewer than three tricks)	opponents score 2 points

The hands shown form a Euchre challenge. Hearts are trumps—and the jack of diamonds is the left bower. Although dealer (right) has four trump cards and nondealer has only three, nondealer can still win three tricks. If nondealer leads ♠K, dealer takes the trick with ♥8. Dealer then leads the left bower, ♦J, and nondealer takes it with ♥J. Nondealer leads ♦7, and dealer takes it with ♥9. No matter which card dealer leads now, the remaining two tricks are nondealer's.

TIPS

The trump suit has nine cards, but there are only seven cards in the other suit of the same color. The two remaining suits have eight cards each. Since each deal leaves out about a third of the deck, on average only five or six cards of each suit are in play. If you have three cards in the trump suit and your partner can take a trick, you are likely to win the majority of tricks.

When you have three practically certain winning cards in your hand and chances of winning the other cards, it may be wise to play alone. Your nontrump cards, even if not clear winners, may take tricks anyway: Your opponents have only ten cards between them and may fail to hold on to the right cards!

Don't forget that if the upcard is accepted as trumps, it becomes part of the dealer's hand. This may influence your decision to accept that suit as trumps for your side.

The game score may also influence your decision to pass, accept, or play alone. If you have a large lead, it may be a good risk to venture a questionable acceptance of the trump suit if you fear an opponent may score a march (4 points) in a different suit. Even if you're euchred, opponent scores only 2 points.

VARIATION

Two-Handed Euchre is generally played with a 24-card pack, omitting 7s and 8s as well. Score for a march is 2 points.

FAN TAN

Fan Tan, an easy game to learn, is also known as
Card Dominoes, Sevens, and Parliament.

♣ ♦ ♠ ♥

PLAYERS

Three to eight, but the game is best when four play

OBJECT

To be the first to play off all your cards

CARDS

Use a regular pack of 52 cards. Aces are low.

PLAYING

Give each player an equal supply of chips; you'll need a bowl or a
dish to collect chips for the kitty. Deal one card at a time to each
player, until the whole pack is dealt. It doesn't matter if some
players have one card fewer than the others.

Beginning with the player at the dealer's left, each player must play a 7, or else add on to cards in suit sequences ascending or descending from the 7s. Once the ♦7 has been played, for example, the ♦8 or ♦6 can be played. If the ♦8 is played, you can play the ♦9, and so on. Sequences ascend to the king and descend to the ace. Once an end card is reached, fold up the row of cards and turn them over.

Whenever you don't have a card to play, pass and toss one chip into the kitty. Whoever is out of cards first collects the chips in the kitty, plus one chip per card left in each player's hand.

TIPS

Try to encourage play in suits where you have aces or kings. Your goal is to be able to hold back stoppers: The 5s, 6s, 8s, and 9s that block everyone else's cards but not your own. If your timing is right, the suits you need help in will open up before your stoppers are gone.

See the following page for an example of a Fan Tan game set up.

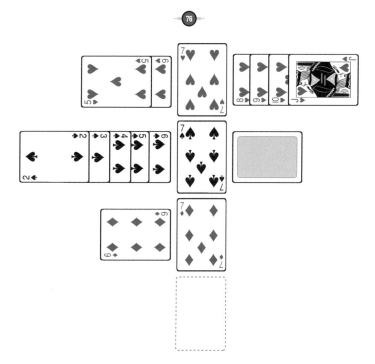

A Fan Tan game in progress. The sequence of high ♠s has already been completed and the cards turned over. The empty spot indicates where the ♣7 will go when that suit is started.

GO FISH

For many of us, Go Fish was the first card game we learned to play, and for some of us, it may still be the one we play best!

♣ ◆ ♠ ♥

PLAYERS

Two to six

OBJECT

To win the most sets of four cards (books) by asking other players for them

CARDS

Use a regular pack of 52 cards, or shorten the game by removing all the cards of a few different ranks.

PLAYING

When two people play, deal seven cards each; otherwise, deal five cards each. Leave the undealt cards facedown as a draw pile. Starting with the player at the dealer's left, each player asks another for cards of a specific rank. For example: "Kevin, do you have any 6s?" In order to ask, you yourself must already have at least one 6. Kevin has to give you all the 6s he currently holds, but the other players do not.

Whenever your request for a card is filled, it remains your turn. Continue with your turn, asking any player for cards of a specific rank. When the player you ask can't oblige, you'll be told to "Go fish." Pick up the top card of the draw pile. If it's the rank you called for, show the card at once, and your turn goes on. Otherwise, your turn ends.

Play proceeds to the left in this fashion. Whenever you have collected all four cards of one rank (a book), show the other players, then place the book next to you in a pile.

SCORING

When all the cards have been drawn and all the books collected, whoever has the most books wins.

TIP

Pay attention to who seeks which cards, because you will almost certainly draw a card someone was looking for earlier. You'll capture those cards at your next turn if you can remember which player to ask!

VARIATIONS

Call for cards from all players at once: Play moves faster when everyone must give up the wanted cards. This also makes it a better move to ask for a card when your book lacks just one, since whoever might have drawn it must give it to you.

An interesting scoring variant is to give each book a value equal to its rank. Aces count 11, face cards 10, and others face value.

With this hand, you can ask for 2s, Qs, 10s, 3s, or 4s.

HEARTS

In any of its numerous variations, Hearts is not difficult to play, but it's certainly not easy to master. An observant and calculating player will be a consistent winner.

♣ ♦ ♠ ♥

PLAYERS

Two to six, but four is the best number for those who enjoy tactical play.

OBJECT

To either win as few of the penalty cards as possible (all the hearts as well as the ♠Q), or else to win them all.

CARDS

Use a standard 52-card deck. There is no trump suit. Cards rank from ace (high) to 2 (low).

DEALING

All cards are dealt clockwise. With four players, each player gets 13 cards. If there are three players, discard the ♦2, leaving 51 cards in the deck, so that each player gets 17. If more than four players, get rid of the lowest clubs so that every player has the same number of cards. For example, if five play, discard the ♣2 and ♣3. This way, each player will have ten cards.

PASSING

In the pass, each player sends three cards to another player. (In a three-player game, pass four.) A popular method is to pass the cards to the left on the first deal, to the right on the second deal, and across on the third deal, with no pass at all on the fourth deal. The cycle then repeats. Players may not look at the cards passed to them until they have completed their own pass.

In this hand, it's a good idea to pass the ♠Q, since only one spade protects it in this hand. Also, pass the ♥Q, which is likely to take a trick with several hearts, and the singleton ♣A, so you can discard high cards or hearts when clubs are led.

PLAYING

The player with the lowest club must lead it to the first trick. The play continues clockwise. The next player must follow suit if possible. If the suit can't be followed, play any card except a penalty card—hearts and the ♠Q cannot be played on the first hand. Whoever plays the highest card of the suit led wins the trick and leads to the next trick.

BREAKING HEARTS

After the first trick, a heart can be "dumped" on the trick if you are out of the suit led, which is called "breaking hearts." Hearts can't be led until after a heart has been played as a discard to another trick, unless it's your lead and you have only hearts left.

After the first trick, the ♠Q can also be "dumped" on the trick if you are out of the suit led.

SCORING

At the end of the hand, all the hearts and the ♠Q are tallied, with each heart scoring one point and the ♠Q scoring 13 points. Count the penalty points for the scoring cards among all the tricks you've won. For example, if you have ♥2, ♥5, ♥9, ♥T, ♥Q, and the ♠Q, your score is 18 points.

The one exception is when you "Shoot the Moon," that is, when you take all the hearts and the ♠Q, in which case you can choose to have either all your opponents assessed 26 points or your running total reduced by 26 points. The game continues until one player has reached or exceeded 100 points at the conclusion of a hand.

TIPS

You generally want to avoid taking tricks; however, on most hands, you'll take a few. In fact, sometimes you may want to take a trick if you think one of your opponents is trying to shoot the moon! Your main concern is always to avoid the trick that includes the ♠Q. This especially affects the pass.

If you are dealt the ♠Q, you may be safer keeping it if you have several other spades to protect it. Otherwise it may be a danger in your hand and you should pass it, for the other players will lead spades. The ♠A and ♠K are risky to keep when you are short in spades since they may be forced to capture the dreaded ♠Q. Spades lower than the ♠Q are very safe to keep, since none of them can capture the ♠Q for your hand.

Also, use the pass to get rid of high cards in short suits or to void suits so you can discard during play.

The first trick is a great way to discard your highest-ranking clubs without worry about getting stuck with hearts or the ♠Q. If you don't have any clubs, it can be a good opportunity to dump the ♠A or ♠K of spades, or high cards in other suits.

If you know that you will be forced to take a trick, take it with the highest card possible, so as to keep your lower cards in that suit available for a different hand.

Of course, if you want to "Shoot the Moon," modify these tips accordingly. For example, void suits if possible, and do not keep any hearts that may lose to a heart trick.

VARIATIONS

Because Hearts is played in many different ways, be certain that the rules are set prior to play. Here are just some of the many variations:

Some players do not want to have passing as an element in the game.

Some consider playing the ♠Q to count as breaking hearts as well.

In some games, the ♠Q be dumped at the first opportunity so favoritism isn't possible.

Another variation is that the player to the left of the dealer leads and not the player with the lowest club.

Some variations count either the ♦10 or ♦J as –5 or –10.

TWO-HANDED HEARTS

This streamlined version for two players of the popular four-handed game retains a lot of the sport of the original.

♣ ♦ ♠ ♥

PLAYERS

Two

OBJECT

To get the lower score. Hearts taken in tricks count 1 each, and the ♠Q counts 6. Or you can shoot the moon, which means you take all the hearts plus the ♠Q and score 19 for the other player.

CARDS

A regular pack of 52 cards is used. Aces are high.

PLAYING

Deal 13 cards to each player, one at a time. Put the remainder of the pack face down as the stock. Unlike the four-handed game,

Two-Handed Hearts does not permit exchanging cards before play. Nondealer leads to the first trick.

You must follow suit if you are able to; otherwise, play any card. No suit is trump. The trick is taken by the higher card of the suit that is led. After each trick, both players take a new card from the stock, the winner of the trick drawing first.

Hearts may not be led until a heart has been discarded. Of course, should you have nothing but hearts, you must play one.

Although in four-handed Hearts, people often use the rule that the ♠Q must be discarded at the first opportunity, the two-handed version doesn't require it. The reason for the rule when more people are playing is to forestall charges of favoritism; this complaint can't arise in a two-handed game.

However, one common rule is that if a player leads the ♠A, opponent must follow with the queen if able to. If a player leads ♠K, opponent also must follow with the queen or else win the trick with the ace if either is possible.

Play continues until all tricks have been played out, even after the stock has been exhausted.

SCORING

Players count the hearts in the tricks they have taken and score a point for each. The player who took the ♠Q in a trick scores 6 points. Low score wins after ten hands. A successful moon shot scores 19 points for the other player.

TIPS

You usually want to avoid taking tricks. When you win a trick, use a high card. When you lose a trick, also use a high card—for example, play the ♣10 under the ♣J.

Deuces are especially valuable, for they let you lose the lead as long as your opponent can follow suit. Of course, once the deuce is played, the 3 becomes low in that suit.

If you void yourself in a suit, you can discard the ♠Q when that suit is led. As long as you have the queen, hold other spades as protection against your opponent's spade leads. If you do not have the ♠Q and suspect that your opponent may, lead spades lower than the queen.

To shoot the moon, a player will need enough high hearts to win every heart trick. Don't let opponent's hearts become too strong by discarding the wrong heart. You always have to sacrifice and win at least a heart or two to stop a moon shot (unlike in four-handed Hearts, where you can always hope that someone else will take the fall).

VARIATIONS

All the variants that you can consider for four-handed Hearts can be incorporated in this game as well. You can incorporate a number of variants.

I DOUBT IT

I Doubt It is a hilarious game that's fun for children as well as adults. If you have a suspicious mind, this game is for you.

♣ ◆ ♠ ♥

PLAYERS

Two or more, but it's a greater challenge with at least three.

OBJECT

To be the first player to get rid of all your cards

CARDS

Use a regular pack of 52 cards for two to five players. Use two packs of 52 cards for six or more players.

PLAYING

Deal all the cards out, as evenly as possible. To save time, deal in twos or threes. In turn, players discard one or more cards, announcing them by rank. Start with aces. The player at the dealer's left begins by saying, for example, "Two aces" and placing two cards facedown in the center of the table to begin a discard stack.

The next player announces "Deuces"—or perhaps, "One deuce"—and puts a single card facedown on the stack. Lay successive discard packets crosswise to keep them distinct from each other. The next player announces "3s" and so on, each player stating a rank just above the previous one. After you reach kings, start again at aces.

During your turn, you must discard, but the cards you discard don't have to be the rank declared. You might announce "Three queens" and discard two jacks and a 6, or any other three cards. Be convincing! Anyone can challenge you by being first to shout, "I doubt it!"

CHALLENGES

If challenged, turn over your discards. If they're not what you said, you must pick up the entire discard pack. But if you told the truth, your challenger picks up the stack!

When you use a single pack, you can discard four cards. With two decks, the discard can go up to eight cards.

TIPS

You'll often need to make a phony discard. This may be easier to do when the discard stack is low. At this time, you may get away with a one-card lie. As the pile grows, so do the risks of discarding and challenging. You're sure to be challenged on your final discard. So plan ahead to have at least one card of the rank you'll need. It can even be helpful to expand your hand by losing an occasional challenge.

VARIATION

In some games, there may be too many challenges, and you may want to bring order to them. One way to do this is to permit only the next player to say "I doubt it."

Lay successive discard packets crosswise to avoid disputes. Here, a player who announced 3 kings has been caught playing two 5s and a jack.

KALUKI

Spell it Kalooki, Caloochi, or Kalogghi, this double-deck Rummy game has been a longtime club favorite in America and Great Britain.

♣ ♦ ♠ ♥

PLAYERS

Two to six

OBJECT

To be the first player to go out, that is, get rid of all the cards in your hand by creating melds.

CARDS

Two regular packs of 52 cards plus their four jokers are used. Jokers can be used to stand for any other card.

PLAYING

With two to four players, deal 15 cards each. With five players, deal 13 each, and with six, deal 11 each. Then turn one card up to start the discard pile. The remaining cards form the stock. A player cannot take the upcard until he or she has made an initial meld or can use the upcard immediately in a meld. Your first meld must total at least 51 points, which can include cards you lay off on other players' melds, keeping in mind that you have to table at least one meld of your own.

MELDS

Melds are three or more cards of the same rank (no repeated suits), or three or more cards of the same suit in sequence. Aces can be high or low, but not both. For example, ♦Q-♦K-♦A and ♦A-♦2-♦3 are valid melds, but ♦K-♦A-♦2 is not.

Ace	15 points
Face card	10 points
Plain card	face value
Joker	value of the card it stands for
Jokers melded as a group	15 points each

Before your initial meld, when it is your turn, either take the upcard if you can meld it or else take the top card from stock, meld if able, and discard. After your initial meld, you are entitled to pick the card showing and discard from your hand without melding. Whenever you meld, you may also lay off cards on your own and other players' melds.

SCORING

Each losing player pays the winner 1 point per card left in hand and 2 points per joker left in hand.

TIPS

It usually doesn't take many rounds for someone to go out, so there's no real advantage to delaying your initial meld. Jokers are valuable. While they can be melded as a group for 15 points each, they are put to much better use individually.

VARIATIONS

In scoring, an alternate practice is to penalize players for the face value of the cards in their hand, with jokers counting 25 points each. One version of Kaluki counts aces as 11, not 15, so agree among the players about this beforehand. A player who goes out on a single play goes Kaluki and collects double points from every player.

KLABERJASS

Try pronouncing this game "Klobber-yosh"—or just call it
Klob. Probably Hungarian in origin, it became a favorite for
gamblers in the United States as a one-on-one test of talent.

♣ ♦ ♠ ♥

PLAYERS

Two

OBJECT

To score points by declaring sequences and by winning high-
scoring cards in tricks.

CARDS

A 32-card deck, A-K-Q-J-10-9-8-7 for each suit. The rank of
trump cards is different from that in the other suits. Card rank in
trumps: J (high), 9, A, 10, K, Q, 8, 7. Card rank in the other suits:
A, 10, K, Q, J, 9, 8, 7.

PLAYING

Deal six cards to each player, one at a time, and turn over an upcard to propose trump.

Nondealer speaks first, saying "Pass," "Take," or "Schmeiss" (pronounced "shmice").

Take means nondealer accepts the suit turned up as trump, becoming the maker, or player responsible for making the higher score.

Schmeiss is an offer to throw the hand in. If dealer accepts, the cards are thrown in for a new deal. If dealer refuses, the schmeisser must become the maker with the upcard suit as trump.

If nondealer passes, dealer then must pass, accept, or schmeiss.

If you both pass on the first round, nondealer names a new trump suit or passes again. If the latter, dealer now names a new trump suit or passes If both pass twice, the hand is thrown in, with no redeal; the deal alternates in Klaberjass.

Once a suit has been settled on for trumps, each player is then dealt another three cards, bringing the hands to nine cards. At this time it's also customary to turn up the bottom card of the deck.

If the original upcard was accepted as trump, either player with the 7 of trump may now exchange it for the upcard.

Your opponent (on left) passes, but you should take up, planning to exchange the ♥7 for the ♥A. You'll have the three highest trumps, guaranteeing 45 points, and you are likely able to win last trick too. If the three cards you draw contain any other trumps or aces, you will do very well.

SEQUENCES

Before playing out the tricks, determine which player, if either, has the highest sequence. Only the player with the highest-ranking sequence may score for sequences. For sequences only, each suit follows the order A-K-Q-J-10-9-8-7 Three or more cards in a row, all of the same suit, form a sequence.

A three-card sequence is worth 20 points; a four-card or longer sequence is worth 50 points. A 50-point sequence is higher than a 20-point sequence. Between sequences of equal value, the one with the higher top card is higher. If the sequences tie in rank, a sequence in trump beats one not in trump. If neither sequence is trump, nondealer's sequence beats dealer's.

Nonmaker begins the dialogue, claiming "20" or "50" or "no sequence." Maker now answers, either declaring "no sequence," or agreeing that nonmaker's meld is "good," or, if the sequences have equal value, by asking, "How high?"

The player whose sequence is high may also declare any other sequence, regardless of its value or rank. To score your sequences, you must show them before playing to the second trick. The other player scores no sequences.

Once the sequences dialogue is over, play begins. No matter who the maker is, nondealer always makes the first lead. Thereafter, the winner of a trick leads to the next one.

A trick is won by the higher trump in it or, if it has no trump, by the higher card. You must follow suit if able. If unable to follow suit, you must trump if possible; otherwise, you may discard. If a trump is led, you must play a higher trump if able.

SCORING

Each player earns points by taking certain cards in tricks.

Jack of trump (Jass, pronounced "yahss")	20
9 of trump (Menel, pronounced "muh-NIL")	14
Each ace	11
Each 10	10
Each king	4
Each queen	3
Each jack (not trump)	2
Last trick	10

BELLA

If you hold the K-Q of trump, declare 20 points for Bella when you play the second of them to a trick.

Players combine their trick score with any sequences or Bella. If maker's total is greater than defender's, then both record their points. If maker and defender tie, defender's score only is recorded. If defender scores more than maker, credit defender with both scores. First player to 500 points wins.

TIPS

You won't always have a rock-crusher of a hand in the first six cards. The last three cards received can be high trumps and nice cards for sequences, or useless losers, or a mix of the good and the bad. If you become the maker needing to fill in an open sequence, you probably won't get it. With two sequences open, your chances improve a good deal.

J-Q-K or J-9-A of trump is an obvious take, but you may want to take with J-Q of trump plus some high tricks. Jack alone with two outside tricks is a very reasonable take. Also, to accept with A-K-Q of trump (40 points with Bella) and an outside ace will usually win—unless opponent has very high trumps or a 50 sequence.

The schmeiss is a unique feature of Klaberjass. As nondealer, schmeiss when you have only a fair chance to win with the trump proposed and fear opponent may make a big score picking a different suit for trumps. Otherwise, pass and name a good suit later.

When nondealer passes, dealer should accept or schmeiss if possible rather than allowing opponent to name a new trump suit.

If opponent is nearing 500 and you are rather behind, don't become maker unless you have a chance to win big. Otherwise opponent will score enough points simply as defender.

VARIATIONS

Some players allow nondealer a schmeiss on the second round, after two passes. For instance, "Schmeiss clubs" leaves dealer the choice to either throw the hand in or be the defender with clubs as trump. Dealer cannot schmeiss on the second round.

KINGS IN THE CORNER

Here's a snappy game that feels like everybody's playing a single solitaire—but there's only one winner!

♣ ♦ ♠ ♥

PLAYERS

Two to six

OBJECT

To go out by playing off all your cards.

CARDS

One pack of 52 cards, plus a supply of pennies or chips.

PLAYING

Deal each player seven cards, then turn four cards face up to start layoff piles. (One king will go in each corner space shown in the diagram.) Place the remaining cards face down in the center as a draw pile.

Player at dealer's left goes first, and subsequent play moves clockwise. If you make no play, pay a chip into the pool. Otherwise, play any number of cards, as long as the plays are valid. At the end of your turn, whether you made any plays or not, draw a new card—except if you go out!

These moves are valid:

1. Playing a king in a corner.

2. Playing a card one rank lower and of opposite color on the top card of any pile. (In other words, these piles have alternating colors.) Ace is the lowest card.

3. Moving an entire layoff pile onto another, if the bottom card of the pile moved is one lower and of the opposite color than the card you are moving it to. This may occur during your turn or as a result of the deal. For example, in the layout shown, the first player can move the ♥7 onto the ♣8. A king dealt to the layout can be moved into the corner by the first player.

4. Playing any card onto a layoff space that has become empty during play.

If you play your last card during your turn, you win.

SCORING

At the end of the game, losers pay 10 chips for each king they hold, while every other card costs one chip. Winner collects all the chips. If you prefer to score on paper, omit the penalty chips paid for passes.

TIPS

Although you may have several plays to make on one turn, it may be wise to save some plays for a later round. First, if you save a play for a future round, it may spare you from paying a chip to the pool. Second, by holding back a card, you may prevent the next players from making plays they might otherwise make.

KNAVES

Looking for an entertaining game to play when you don't have a foursome? Here's an easy game for three.

♣ ♦ ♠ ♥

PLAYERS

Three

OBJECT

To win as many tricks as possible, but to avoid winning jacks (knaves).

CARDS

One 52-card pack. Aces are high.

PLAYING

Deal 17 cards to each player and turn the last card up as trump. Player at dealer's left leads to the first trick. Follow suit whenever possible; otherwise trump or play any other card; you are not required to trump if you don't have the suit led.

The winner of a trick leads to the next trick.

SCORING

After all 17 tricks have been played, score one point for each trick taken. For each jack taken, you subtract points as shown.

♥J	-4
♦J	-4
♣J	-2
♠J	-1

The first to reach a score of 21 wins.

TIP

When you play second to a trick in a suit where the jack is still out, playing the Q, K, or A is taking a big chance. But as third and last to play, you may want to win a trick with the Q, K, or A—even when you could do so with a much lower card. This saves you the risk of taking the jack on a later play.

VARIATION

Some use a rule that when the turned-up trump card is a jack, it goes to the winner of the last trick.

MICHIGAN

The many names of this game—Chicago, Saratoga, Newmarket, Stops, Boodle, and others—show its far-reaching appeal.

♣ ♦ ♠ ♥

PLAYERS

Three to eight

OBJECT

To win chips by being the first player out of cards and by playing money or boodle cards.

CARDS

A regular pack of 52 cards is used, plus an extra ♥A, ♣K, ♠Q, and ♦J (the boodle cards). Aces are high.

PLAYING

Distribute an equal number of chips to each player. (Number agreed upon by players). Place the four boodle cards face up in the center of the table, where they remain throughout play. Each player puts one chip on each boodle card except the dealer, who places two chips on each.

Deal all the cards out, one at a time, dealing one hand more than there are players. The extra hand, called the widow, is dealt to dealer's left. It's all right if some players have one more card than the others.

As dealer, look at your cards and decide if you wish to exchange them for the widow (without seeing it first). If you prefer, keep your original hand and auction the widow, still unseen, to the other players. The auction begins at one chip. The high bidder wins the widow hand and must play it and pay the dealer.

This hand lacks boodle cards, high cards, and aces. Consider swapping it for the widow.

The player at dealer's left leads the lowest card held of any suit. Whoever has the next card in sequence in that suit plays it, and so on, until no one can play. For example, the ♥4 is led, the same player also plays the ♥5, and then other players follow with the ♥6, ♥7, and ♥8. No one has the ♥9, a stopper, so whoever played the ♥8 now continues play, leading the lowest card of a different suit.

When an ace is played, the sequence ends. Begin a new sequence with your lowest card in another suit. Whenever you play a boodle card, collect the chips on it. If you play your last card, the deal ends and you win; collect one chip from each player for every card remaining in their hand. The deal also ends when no one can continue the sequence and the last player lacks another suit to lead.

Leave all uncollected chips on the boodle cards. The deal passes to the left, and all players put another chip on each boodle card. Since the dealer has an advantage, the game ends after an agreed number of complete dealing rounds. Whoever has the most chips is the winner.

TIP

If you take the widow, remember the cards you threw away. This can help a lot in the play.

VARIATIONS

One version of Michigan requires that players pay an extra penalty if they are caught at the end holding a boodle card.

Another variant adds a fifth boodle, usually the sequence ♥9-♥10-♥J. Anyone playing two of these cards in a row collects their boodle chips. You can always use an A-K-Q-J of different suits for boodle cards, but if you use the 9-10-J sequence boodle, it should be the same suit as the ace.

In Oh Hell! it's not how good your cards are, but how good your luck and judgment are. The game does have its momentary upsets, so if you need a name that's a bit more tame, just call it "Oh Well!"

♣ ♦ ♠ ♥

PLAYERS

Three to seven; however, the game is best with four or five players. One player acts as scorekeeper.

OBJECT

To make precisely the number of tricks you bid—no more and no less.

CARDS

A regular pack of 52 cards is used. Aces are high.

PLAYING

A game of Oh Hell! consists of a series of rounds. On the first, deal each player one card; on the second, deal two cards; and on the third, deal three, increasing the deal by one card each hand until the top limit. For example, when four people play, deal 13 cards on the last round. With five players, deal ten cards on the last round. The deal goes to the left for each new round.

After dealing, turn up one card to designate trumps. If you turn over an ace or a deuce, however, play at no-trump, with no suit as trumps. Also, whenever you deal all 52 cards, play at no-trump.

BIDDING

Starting at dealer's left, players state in turn the number of tricks they hope to win. The scorekeeper records each bid. The total number of tricks bid for on each deal must differ from the number of tricks available. Therefore, the scorer must require the last bidder—the dealer—to register a legal bid.

Once all the bids are recorded, the player at dealer's left leads any card desired. Always follow suit if possible, but play any card otherwise. Each trick is taken by the highest card in the suit led or by the highest trump. The winner of each trick leads to the following trick.

SCORING

After all the tricks have been taken, the scorekeeper tallies how everyone fared. If you made your bid exactly, score 1 point per trick plus a 10-point bonus. If you failed, however, subtract 10 points for each trick you're off, whether it's more or less than your bid. The player with the most points after the last deal wins.

TIPS

Bidding in the first few rounds can be tricky, since so few cards from the pack are in play, and some bids are forced. In the early deals, you'll be surprised to see your low cards win tricks, while your aces get trumped. In most deals, you can count on low cards to be losers more reliably than counting on high cards to be winners.

When the bid total is above the number of tricks in the deal, other players will be quite willing to capture your questionable middle-range cards or trump a trick in which you played a high card. When the bid total is under the trick total, players will let you win an extra trick or two.

VARIATIONS

Some players prefer to write down bids secretly. In this case, it's okay for the bid total and the trick total to turn out equal. Those bids can be revealed either before the first lead or after the last trick.

In many games, once the highest possible number of cards have been dealt, the game continues with the number of cards per hand decreasing by one each hand, until you work your way back down to a final one-card deal.

OLD MAID

Many of us think Old Maid requires a special pack of cards, but actually its ancestral form some 150 years ago likely used a regular pack minus one card.

♣ ♦ ♠ ♥

PLAYERS

Three or more is best, though two can play.

OBJECT

Not to be left holding the Old Maid.

CARDS

A pack of 51 cards is used, made by removing one queen from a regular pack.

PLAYING

Deal all the cards out one at a time. Before play starts, each player shows and retires any pairs of like rank. After that, the player at dealer's left takes one card, unseen, from the player at his or her left. If this makes a pair, it is also tabled, and the player continues, taking a card from the next player to the left. When the card taken does not make a pair, play passes on to the next player, who in turn takes a card from the next player.

In this way all cards eventually pair up except one queen, and the player holding it is declared Old Maid.

TIP

After one pair of queens has been tabled, only body language can tell you who might have the remaining lone queen. Even so, it's hard to know which card that queen might be.

VARIATIONS

Instead of removing a queen, randomly remove one card that no one sees from the pack. In this way, only at the very end will all the players discover which card in actuality was the Old Maid.

For a quicker game, you can shrink the pack by omitting all cards of several ranks.

PINOCHLE

Auction Pinochle is one of the most popular three-player card games in existence. Though the original game of Pinochle is derived from the European game Bezique, Auction Pinochle appears to have been developed in the United States some time during the middle of the 19th century.

♣ ♦ ♠ ♥

PLAYERS

Three (or four, with the dealer sitting out each deal)

OBJECT

To score 1,500 points in melds and in play.

CARDS

A 48-card Pinochle deck is used. You can put one together from two standard decks by dropping all 2s through 8s, leaving just the 9s, tens, jacks, queens, kings, and aces. The cards rank from high to low A, 10, K, Q, J, 9.

PLAYING

One player shuffles all of the cards and deals each of the players one card faceup. The high card deals the first game. After the cards have been reshuffled, the dealer deals 15 cards to each player. Traditionally, cards are dealt in bunches of three, or one bunch of three followed by bunches of four. The dealer deals three cards (not the last three) to a facedown widow, or kitty. The deal rotates one spot to the left after every game.

BIDDING

Starting with the player to the left of the dealer, each player bids or passes. The lowest bid is 250 points, and bids increase by ten points thereafter. Once a player passes, he/she can't reenter the bidding, but bidders can continue raising the auction. The auction is closed once two players have passed. The goal is for the winning bidder to score at least as many points as he/she bid. Players score points by playing melds and winning tricks.

Flush (A, 10, K, Q, J of trumps)	150 points
Royal Marriage (K, Q of trumps)	40 points
Simple Marriage (Plain Marriage) (K, Q of a nontrump suit)	20 points
100 Aces (A of each suit)	100 points
80 Kings (K of each suit)	80 points
60 Queens (Q of each suit)	60 points
40 Jacks (J of each suit)	40 points
Pinochle (♠Q, ♦J)	40 points
Double Pinochle (two ♠Q, two ♦J)	300 points
Dix (pronounced "deece") (9 of trumps)	10 points

Note that if the player declares a flush, he/she may not then declare the marriage contained inside the flush.

The player who wins the bid becomes the bidder. If you win the bid, you must then turn the three cards in the widow hand faceup and add them to your hand.

If at this time it is clear that you cannot reach the bid amount, you may immediately concede the hand and lose the amount of points bid. If you decide to continue, you place all of your melds on the table in front of you and declare which suit is trump. Your meld can include any of the cards from the widow hand. If you have already reached or exceeded the value of the bid, play ceases immediately, and you win points for your bid and cards (see "Scoring" on page 117).

When bidding, you must choose three cards that are not included in any of your melds to set aside in order to reduce your hand back down to 15 cards. The points from these three cards are later added to the tricks won during play. After setting aside your three cards, you can then pick up your melds and lead any card to begin the first hand. At this time, your two opponents will temporarily unite in their play against you and attempt to take tricks to keep you from making your bid.

The winner of each trick leads the next. Players must always follow suit if they can do so. If players cannot follow suit, they must play a trump if possible. After a card is led, each player must play a higher card than the previous player, if possible. Tricks are taken by the highest card of the suit led or by the highest trump. When two of the same card—for example, two aces of clubs—are played to a trick, the card played first is considered the higher of the two.

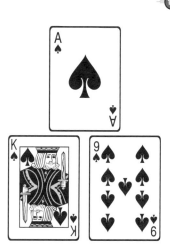

The ace is the high card and wins the trick.

If diamonds are trump, they will beat any of the other cards played.

Once all the tricks have been played, the bidding player adds up his/her points based on the point values below.

Ace	11
Ten	10
King	4
Queen	3
Jack	2
Nine	0
Last trick	10

SCORING

If you are the bidder and you make your bid, you can collect points from each opponent according to the scoring table to the right. If you concede, you lose points to each opponent according to the scoring table. If you act as the bidder and play, yet still miss your bid, you lose double to each opponent for going bête (pronounced "bait").

Bid	Points
250–290	5
300–340	10
350–390	15
400–440	25
450–490	50
500+	100

For bids over 300, spades score double.

Here is an example of scoring to make it easier to understand. Player A wins the bid and becomes bidder with 370 and makes 405 in spades. Player A receives 30 points from each opponent. If Player A had bid 400 and made 405 in spades, he/she would win 50 from each opponent. But, if Player A had bid 410 and made only 405, he/she would go bête in spades and lose 100 points to each opponent.

TIPS AND STRATEGY

When bidding, a player can reasonably count on the widow to add 20 points to the playing value of his/her hand. However, don't expect the widow to fill any gaps in your hand for melding purposes unless you have at least five gaps to fill. There is slightly better than a one-in-six chance that one particular card will be in the widow to give you the points you may be considering, hence the requirement of five gaps. In calculating the points that may be lost in play, it is usually safe to assume that each opponent may put a high card on your losing tricks. See the chart that includes the odds of filling open places in possible melds with the widow.

BIDDING ODDS

Places Open	Approximate Odds
1	5 to 1 against
2	2 to 1 against
3	Even
4	3 to 2 for
5	2 to 1 for

When bidding, you should play the hand instead of conceding unless the odds are two to one against making the bid. When spades count double, as the bidder you should play the hand unless you have worse than even odds against completing the bid. When you are bidding and trying to choose cards to bury in the three cards you set aside, the first choice should be a weak short holding of less than four cards that does not include an ace. Always save your entire longest side suit if possible. You may also consider burying one or two 10s in order to save them from going to your opponents, if it is determined that this is a real possibility based on the contents of the rest of your hand.

One of the most common types of hands played by the bidder is one that holds five or more trumps with a side suit containing four or more cards. In this case, the player should play any aces that are of the other two suits and then lead to the side suit until it is no longer possible. This may very well force the opponents to waste trump on these tricks, weakening their trump position while also possibly forcing them to waste a trump on a trick that their partner would have won.

For defenders, the best plan is to remember the cards that the bidder has melded that can be beat. Defenders should plan to

take these cards. It sometimes takes planning ahead in the hand
to hold on to the cards required to beat the bidder. Occasionally,
the bidder will have even more cards of that suit in his hand, as a
side suit in addition to trumps.

VARIATIONS

Bidding practices have their own traditions. In one, after two
passes the dealer must take with a bid of at least 250. In another,
the dealer passes out the hand or opens it at 290 (but not at 250)
or at 320 or higher. A third treatment requires the first hand
to start at 300, and it is allowed to throw the hand in for the
minimum-stake loss.

This four-player version of Pinochle, sometimes called
Racehorse Pinochle, includes an auction.

♣ ♦ ♠ ♥

PLAYERS

Four, playing as two pairs, with partners sitting opposite each
other.

OBJECT

To be the first team to score 1,500 points.

CARDS

A 48-card Pinochle deck is used.

PLAYING

Deal 12 cards to each player. Bidding starts at dealer's left. Bid or
pass at your turn. The first bid must be at least 250, and any following bids must be a higher multiple of 10. If you pass, you may

bid at a later time, but three consecutive passes end the auction. Whoever made the highest bid becomes the declarer.

If all players pass, throw the hand in, unless you've decided in advance that the dealer takes it for 250 whenever the first three players pass.

Declarer names the trump suit and then receives four cards from partner. Declarer looks them over and returns four cards—which could include some of those received. Finally, all players table any melds they hold, which are then tallied for each side.

For example, you have won the bid at 350 with ♥A-10-9, ♠A-K-Q, ♦A-J, ♣A-A-Q-J, and named clubs trump. Partner passes you the ♦J, ♥A, ♣10-J. Return to partner ♦J, ♠K-Q,♥9, worth 60 in meld, leaving you with a powerful playing hand: ♥A-A-10, ♦A-J, ♠A, ♣A-A-10-Q-J-J.

Even if your melds total only 160, you should have no problem taking 190 in play. Since Pinochle has 250 points available in play, if the declaring side is more than 250 points away from its bid, it cannot possibly fulfill it. The bid is automatically set—the declaring side's melds are erased, and opponents score the value of their melds plus a 250-point bonus. Even when the bid may be within reach, declarer (without consulting partner) may decide not to play on and take an automatic set instead.

If the hand is played but the declaring side's combined total of points in melds and play falls short of the bid, then the contract is also set. In this case the declaring side's melds and trick points are erased, while opponents score their melds and the 250-point set bonus, plus whatever points they took in tricks. If the contract is fulfilled, then both sides score all their points.

TIPS

You'll probably need to achieve 80 or more melding points to make any bid, and much of this depends upon how the hands wind up after the card exchange. Before sitting down, players can discuss their exchange strategies and decide what type of cards high bidder's partner should send.

VARIATION

Partnership Pinochle without an auction is also quite popular. Trump is determined by turning the last card up as trumps, which becomes part of dealer's hand. Players table their melds, and then player to dealer's left makes the first play. Each side scores the points it makes in tricks and melds. First side to 1,500 wins.

An old tradition in Partnership Pinochle is that your side must take at least one trick to score its melds.

TWO-HANDED PINOCHLE

Two-Handed Pinochle was probably the most popular card game
for two in the United States before Gin Rummy.

♣ ♦ ♠ ♥

PLAYERS

Two

OBJECT

To score the most points by melding and by taking tricks.

CARDS

A 48-card Pinochle deck is used.

PLAYING

Deal 12 cards to each player; turn the next card up to designate
the trump suit. If it's a 9, dealer scores an immediate 10 points.
The remaining cards form a stock pile.

Every deal has two phases: trick-taking with melding and the endgame. To begin the first phase, nondealer leads any card; dealer

may follow by playing any card—you don't have to follow suit. Each trick is won by the higher trump, or if it contains no trump, by the higher card of the suit led. If the two cards are identical, the first one played wins.

Winner of the trick tables any one of the Pinochle melds. Though a player may hold more than one meld in hand, only one melding combination may be tabled after winning a trick. Another trick must be won to make the second meld. This does not apply to the 9s of trump. The first dix can be exchanged for the upcard to get a higher trump. The second is simply shown to opponent and the 10 points scored.

A melded card may be used again in a different meld. For example, the ♠Q may be melded with the ♠K in a marriage; when a later trick is won, the same ♠Q may be melded with a ♦J in a pinochle or with ♣Q-♥Q-♦Q for 60 queens. A second marriage in spades would require a new ♠Q and ♠K. Cards melded on the table still belong to the hand of their owner and may be played to any trick. However, cards taken in tricks are out of play for the rest of the hand.

After a trick is won and any meld tabled, both players take a new card from the stock. Winner of the trick draws first and leads to the next trick.

ENDGAME

When only the upcard and a single stock card are left, the winner of the trick takes the stock card, and the loser takes the upcard (which at this point will be the 9 of trump). No further melds may be made. Players return to their hands any cards melded on the table, and the winner of the last trick starts the endgame by leading any card.

In playing the tricks during the endgame, a player must follow suit if able; otherwise, the player must trump if able. When a trump is led, opponent must play a higher trump if able. The object is to take tricks with high-scoring cards. Game is usually played to 1,000 points. If both players reach over 1,000 points on the same deal, the higher total wins.

TIPS

Cards played to tricks in the first phase of the game are no longer available for melding. Play a possible melding card only if you're sure you can spare it.

Kings and queens (especially the ♠Q) are good melding cards. Retain these cards while the possibility of melding with them is still alive. Jacks are not valuable cards to keep for melding (except the ♦J). Four different jacks score only 40 points, so unless you have this meld, don't keep jacks.

If you've seen both ♦Ks, then all other kings become less valuable, since 80 kings is no longer a possible meld.

If your opponent plays a good melding card early, it's likely to be a duplicate. However, they may be missing the rest of the meld and be strapped for a play.

Use a trump in beginning play to meld some cards and free them for play, or to prevent opponent from melding. In the endgame a long trump suit will bring in several extra tricks, as well as the last trick.

In the endgame, beware the singleton ace. If opponent plays the other ace, you follow suit and lose. Play yours first.

POKER

Poker has endless variants, but they fall into three main groups: Draw Poker, Stud Poker, and Texas Hold 'Em Poker.

♣ ♦ ♠ ♥

OBJECT

To win the pot, either by being the only player left or by having the best cards.

GENERAL POKER RULES

These rules apply to all types of Poker games. In any individual game, it's important that all players know the bet limits and the rules. Here are the general rules of play:

Each player receives a stack or stacks of chips. Deal and betting proceed clockwise (to the left). At the showdown (end of the hand) the last to bet—or to raise the bet—shows first. Players calling the final bet have a right to see the cards of all others who call.

If at any point only one player is left, that hand wins and need not be shown.

Rank of hands in Poker: In descending order of rank, these are the hands of Poker.

Name	Description	Example
Royal flush	Five sequential cards of the same suit to the ace	♥10-♥J-♥Q-♥K-♥A
Straight flush	Any five sequential cards of the same suit	♥7-♥8-♥9-♥10-♥J
Four of a kind	All four cards of a rank	♣6-♥6-♦6-♠6
Full house	Three of a kind plus a pair	♥3-♠3-♣3-♦10-♠10
Flush	Any five cards of a suit	♠Q-♠9-♠8-♠5-♠2
Straight	Five cards in sequence, any suits. Ace can be either high or low	♦A-♥2-♣3-♦4-♠5
Three of a kind	Three cards of one rank, the rest unmatched	♠K-♦K-♥K-♣9-♦7
Two pair	Two different pairs of two cards of a rank, the fifth unmatched	♦J-♣J-♥8-♣8-♥5
One pair	Two cards of a rank, the rest unmatched	♦J-♣J-♥8-♣7-♥5
High card	No combination. Aces are high.	♣A-♠7-♥9-♣10-♣4

Between hands of the same type, the higher-ranked hand wins. For example, a flush headed by a jack (♣J-♣9-♣5-♣3-♣2) beats a flush to the 10 (♦10-♦9-♦8-♦5-♦3).

LOWBALL POKER

Lowball Poker can be played in as many styles as high only Poker. There is usually a round of betting, a draw, then another betting round and a showdown. Aces rank low. The hand that ranks as the poorest Poker hand wins. For example, ♠7-♣3-♥9-♦4-♣5 (a 9-low) beats ♠4-♣A-♦2-♠J-♥3 (a jack-low).

Most lowball versions disregard flushes and straights and pay attention only to the number value of the cards, so that 7-6-5-4-3 is a 7-low. When hands competing for low have the same worst cards, look to the next worst card.

HIGH-LOW POKER

In high-low Poker, the best hand and the worst hand divide the pot. Any form of Poker—Draw, Stud, or Hold 'Em—can be played high-low. High-low Poker has a few important differences from other games.

In most split games, players declare, before the showdown, whether they are going high, low, or high and low. In some games, this is done out loud, by going around the table starting with the last raiser or bettor. This reduces some surprises and gives a certain positional advantage from which to play.

A more common practice is to declare silently, but at the same time. This can be done using chips or coins. At a signal, players either put no chips in their hand to go low, one chip in their hand to go high, or two chips to go high and low. In some games, this is the final action, after which the winners and losers are sorted out. In some games these declarations are followed by one more betting round (the drive) that gives bluffers and legitimate hands one more chance to raise the pot. Since one player may have a lock on half the pot, high-low Poker limits raises to three per round.

Most high-low games encourage you to go for high and low on the same deal, if you've got right hand. This is easy in seven-card games, where you can use different sets of cards for each direction you go. In five-card games, it must be clear whether a 2-3-4-5-6 straight can be low, that is, a 6-low. If you go high-low but lose in either direction (high or low), you win nothing.

GENERAL TERMS IN POKER:

Ante: Initial stake each player puts into the pot

Betting in the blind: Betting without seeing your cards

Bluffing: Betting or raising with a weak hand

Broadway: A straight to the ace

Call: To equal a bet made by another player

Check: To pass

Drop (or Fold): To quit a hand

(the) Goods: A real hand, no bluff

Hole cards: In Stud and Hold 'Em, face-down cards

Openers: A good enough card combination to meet a minimum requirement

Pat hand: A hand you don't draw to

Pot: All the bets in the center of the table

Pot limit: A dangerous game, where the bet limit is the sum of chips in the pot

Raise: To equal another's bet and add to it

Sandbag: To check (pass) and later raise in the same round

See a bet: To equal it; call

Sixth street: The last upcard in seven-card stud, before a down-card is dealt

Stand pat: Draw no cards

Trips: Three of a kind

Wheel: Ace through five for low

Wild cards: In some games, dealer may call certain cards wild, that is, they can stand for any other card. Sometimes a joker is added as a wild card. Deuces wild (all four of them) is another popular choice. Another favorite is One-eyes wild (the three face cards in profile: ♦K, ♥J, and ♠J).

Now that we've covered the general rules, let's go into details on some of the most common Poker variations. Once you've tried them out, consider making your own Poker game!

DRAW POKER

One of the best-known forms of the game, Draw Poker has been around for a long time and has fans worldwide.

♣ ♦ ♠ ♥

PLAYERS

Two to seven

CARDS

A regular pack of 52 cards is used.

PLAYING

Each player antes one chip. Cards are dealt one by one until each player has five. The first player then may bet or check, but once a player has bet, each player in turn either folds or sees the bet (or perhaps raises it).

Once all bets and raises have been called, the dealer proceeds to ask each player in turn how many cards they wish to draw. The maximum number of cards a player can draw is three. Each player casts unwanted cards aside, and the dealer deals replacements. Dealer's own draw should be clearly announced; for example, the dealer may state, "Dealer takes two." A player who draws no cards is said to stand pat.

Once players have all received their new cards, the final round of betting takes place, beginning with the player who made the last raise or bet. Most games establish a betting limit, which on the second round is usually double the first. When all bets and raises have again been called, there is a showdown to see whose hand is best. Usually the last bettor shows first, and others may fold their hands if beaten. The remaining players have a right to see all hands that have called.

If all players pass on the first round, throw the hand in. The deal passes to the left, and another round of five cards is dealt. Leave the chips in the pot, as players add another ante.

TIPS

Most fairly serious Poker games should have house rules that all players know in advance of play. For example, many games limit the number of raises in a round to three, unless only two players remain, who can then raise and re-raise each other as they wish. Other matters to clarify ahead of time include misdeals, misstatements of hands, maximum bets, and buying new chips, among other issues. To keep the Poker game friendly, take a few moments to make sure everyone is aware of the rules.

STUD POKER

In Stud Poker, players see some of their opponents' cards,
adding a new strategic element to the game.

♣ ◆ ♠ ♥

PLAYERS

Two to eight

CARDS

A regular pack of 52 cards is used.

PLAYING

In Five-Card Stud Poker, each player antes. Deal one card down
and one up to each player. Players look at their face-down cards.

The player with the highest card showing starts by checking or
by betting. As soon as there's a bet, the players following must, in
turn, either fold or call—or perhaps raise—the bet. Once all bets
are called, the remaining players each receive another upcard.
Another round of betting follows, started by the player with the
best hand showing.

The ♥K is the high card. This player may check or bet. If ♥K bets, then the player with the ♦10 sees the bet or else drops (by turning the ♦10 over), and so on with each player around the table. Since the ♥K was the first king dealt, it has betting priority over the ♠K.

Each round of cards dealt up is followed by a betting round. The final round of bets occurs when all players left in the hand have four upcards. This round of betting should have a higher limit than the previous rounds. Also, if any player shows a pair at any time, the bet limit is raised.

After the final bets, the bettor—or last raiser—is usually first to turn over the hole card. If no one calls the last bet or raise, the winner gathers the pot and isn't obliged to show anyone the winning hand.

VARIATIONS

In Seven-Card Stud Poker, the mechanics work just as in Five-Card Stud Poker, except that two hole cards are dealt before the first upcard. After a fourth upcard is dealt to each player, the next card is again dealt down, in the hole. After this, one more betting round ensues.

Any time a pair is showing, a higher bet limit applies. After the sixth and seventh cards, the higher bet limit also applies. To decide the pot, players use their best five cards out of the seven cards dealt.

TEXAS HOLD 'EM

In the World Series of Poker, as well as smaller
prize events, Texas Hold 'Em is the game they play.

♣ ♦ ♠ ♥

PLAYERS

Two to twelve

OBJECT

Best of any five cards from among the two in your hand (the hole
cards) and five on the board (the community cards).

A regular pack of 52 cards is used.

PLAYING

After each player antes, deal two cards face down to each player
and five cards face down in the center of the table. Starting with
the player at dealer's left, each player may check or bet. Once a
player has made a bet, subsequent players must fold unless they
see—or raise—the bet.

Once all first-round bets are called, the dealer turns over the first three face-down cards. These three cards are called the flop. (The fourth is called the "turn" card; the fifth is the "river" card.)

Whoever was the last bettor starts a new round of betting, after which the dealer turns up one more card (turn) from the center of the table. Another betting round ensues, and then the dealer turns over the last card (river) for a final betting round. After all calls, the showdown occurs.

Players use any combination of their hole cards and the community cards to form the best five-card hand possible. Players can use both of their hole cards and three community cards, one hole card and four community cards, or all five community cards. Because everyone can use the five community cards to form their best hand, players who do usually win only part of the pot. An example is when the board shows ♥A-♥K-♥Q-♥J-♥10. Everyone left in the hand splits the pot as the board shows a royal flush, which is the best hand possible.

BLINDS

Most Hold 'Em Poker games require players to post blinds (initial bets) before any cards are dealt in order to stimulate action. Usually there are two blinds, a small blind and a big blind, in each playing round. The blinds rotate one place to the left each hand. The small blind is to the left of the dealer and acts first in all betting rounds except the first and is usually half the amount of the big blind. The big blind is to the left of the small blind and is usually equal to the minimum bet at whatever limit is being played. On the first round of betting, the big blind acts last since he/she already has a full bet in the pot.

If you are entering an existing Hold 'Em game, you will probably be required to post the big blind in order to play at the table. If your seat is near the big blind on your right, you will probably want to wait until the big blind is at your position. If you are already in a Hold 'Em game and you leave the table and miss the blinds, you will be required to post both blinds in order to resume play, or you can wait until the big blind comes to your position.

STRATEGY

In this section, many of the basic strategies involved in becoming a winning Hold 'Em player are discussed. If you are a new player or a player with some experience looking to take your game to the next level, mastering the concepts in this section will greatly improve your game.

POSITION

The position at which a player starts a hand will have a great bearing on how the hand is played. The best position in Hold 'Em, whether limit, no-limit, or pot-limit, is the dealer position (often called the button). The player with the button is the last to act in each round except for the first round of betting (the big blind acts last in the first round). The reason this is such an advantage is that the button gets to see what everyone else does before he/she has to act. This leads to opportunities to steal a pot with a marginal hand and allows good players to win the maximum amount with their good hand. It also allows the good players to minimize their losses in certain situations.

The worst position is the player to the left of the big blind (often called under-the-gun). Your biggest decision in Hold 'Em is the first one you must make: whether to play a hand or not. On average, profitable players enter the pot with better hands than other players. Before you enter a pot, you want as much information as possible. When under-the-gun, you have no information about what any of the other players are going to do. This puts you at a distinct disadvantage. For these reasons, you can often play weaker hands the closer you get to the button. Let's assume that the small blind is in seat 1, the big blind is in seat 2, and the button is in seat 10. The players in seats 3, 4, and 5 are in early position, seats 6 and 7 are in middle position, and seats 8, 9, and 10 are in late position. You will learn in the next section that some hands can be played in the middle or late positions that should not be played in the early positions.

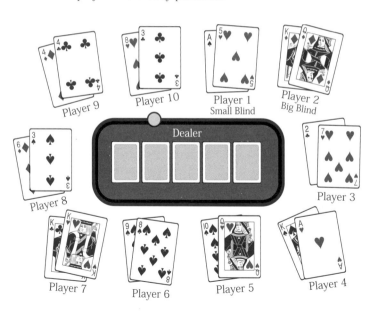

STARTING HAND SELECTION

If your goal is to become a winning Texas Hold 'Em player, this section is invaluable. As stated above, the most important decision you make as a Hold 'Em player is whether or not to enter the pot (or play for the pot).

Almost all losing Hold 'Em players play far too many hands. Winning Hold 'Em players see the flop only between 20 and 25 percent of the time. Let's think about that statement for a minute. Because you will be in the big blind 10 percent of the time, you will often see the flop for free as the big blind. If you are to be a winning player, you won't enter many other pots—only 1½ times on average each round.

Many players will call a half bet in the small blind with any two cards. After reading this book, hopefully you won't play this way as it can cost you considerable money in the long run. This one error, when made repeatedly, can be the difference between winning and losing.

Let's discuss what hands can be played from each position under a variety of circumstances. You should refer to this section often and eventually memorize it as you gain experience. As with everything in poker, rarely is any decision set in stone. The following are solid guidelines to help you understand what to look for in each position. Many things will go into each decision you make, such as who enters the pot before you, whether the pot has been raised, how loose or tight the other players are, and your table image. What is important to remember is that these guidelines are a good starting point, but through experience you will tweak them to best fit your playing style.

Many professional players play more hands than recommended, but their post-flop play and ability to read other players is superior to most people's abilities. This allows them to outplay their opponents and make up for the difference in starting hand composition after the flop.

EARLY POSITION

The following hands are recommended in early position (seats three, four and five):

AA—A pair of aces (hole cards often called pocket rockets) is the best starting hand in any form of Texas Hold 'Em.

Unless you are a seasoned professional, it is recommended to always enter the pot with a raise when you hold a pair of aces. If you raise and are reraised, raise again. This does two things that are favorable for you: It gets as much money as possible in the pot, and it will often force small drawing hands, such as suited connectors (for example ♥3-♥4) and small pairs to fold before the flop. Your goal with pocket rockets is to play either heads-up (only one opponent) or, at the most, against two opponents. Three or more opponents greatly reduce your chances of winning a hand, even if you have the best starting hand.

Pocket Rockets

KK—A pair of kings (often called cowboys) is the second best starting hand in Hold 'Em. Just like pocket aces, you should always raise with pocket kings when you enter a pot. Your goals are the same as with pocket aces with the additional goal of hopefully forcing out opponents who hold an ace with a small kicker. With pocket kings, any flop that contains an ace can be dangerous.

AKs (suited) and AK—The third best starting hand in Texas Hold 'Em is AK whether suited or not. This is one hand that has a rule that is set in stone: You must raise before the flop with AK. You must force as many opponents as possible to fold before the flop when you hold AK. This is a drawing hand and must be protected. Drawing hands must almost always improve to win.

Made hands, such as high pairs like AA, KK, and QQ, will often win even if they don't improve. Of course, you hope to see at least an A or K on the flop whenever you hold AK.

AK, known as Big Slick

QQ—Pocket queens is a strong starting hand. Some players may enter the pot with a raise, and sometimes they will just limp in (call) to see the flop. This is a double-edged sword. You may raise to force out opponents holding an ace with a small kicker or opponents who like to play a king with a suited kicker, or you may limp in and hope that neither an ace nor king is in the flop so you can win extra bets from the above-mentioned opponents. How you play pocket queens depends on how well you know your opponents' playing styles and your position. If a player holds them in middle or late position and is the first one in the pot, they should almost always enter with a raise. Any time you hold them, and an ace or king hits on the flop, you are probably beat, especially against three or more opponents.

JJ—Pocket jacks can be dangerous to inexperienced players. They look good before the flop so many players enter with a raise. The problem is that any ace, king, or queen on the flop forces you to play defensively, and if you face more than one opponent, you are likely to lose.

For this reason, unless you think you can isolate an opponent, you should limp in with pocket jacks. Try to look at pocket jacks the same as any other pair below queens: as a drawing hand.

Of course, if the flop brings nothing higher than a ten, you should bet aggressively until you're convinced that another player has a better hand.

AQs, AQ, AJs, KQs—These hands should be played from any position, even calling a single raise before the flop.

One exception: if a very tight and strong player raises from under-the-gun, then you should consider folding. You should fold everything except AA, KK, and AK if a tight player raises and is reraised before the betting gets to you. Otherwise, these hands are very strong.

When you do hit one of your cards on the flop, opponents will often bet as well (give you action) while holding a smaller kicker. This is the best situation to be in. This is why solid players rarely play aces with kickers below a T, especially from early position.

AJ, ATs, KQ, KJs—Depending on the ability of your opponents, you should often fold these hands when you're under-the-gun. You can play them from the fifth position and sometimes from fourth position as well. These are strong hands, but sometimes an opponent will have a higher kicker when the flop hits you.

MIDDLE POSITION

The following hands are recommended in middle position (seats six and seven):

TT, 99, AT, KJ, QJs—These are drawing hands and will almost always need to improve to win. You should rarely call a raise with these hands. With the pairs (TT and 99), you are hoping to flop a set (three of a kind, also called trips).

The other three hands can and do win when the flop hits you, but even if you have the top pair after the flop, you may not have the top kicker. With these hands, you should often bet after the flop if you do hit something in order to get an idea of where you are in the hand. If you bet and are reraised, depending on the opponent, you usually lose. Often though, this bet after the flop will win the hand, and even if it doesn't, it can set up a bluffing opportunity on the turn.

LATE POSITION

The following hands are recommended in late position (seats eight, nine, and ten):

88, 77, 66, 55, 44, 33, 22—Your main hope is to flop a set with these pairs. As with all of the hands here and below, you should rarely call a raise from a solid player. Most drawing hands prefer to have many opponents so that when you hit your draw, you will be able to collect more than enough money to pay for the times that you don't.

KT, QJ—These two hands usually need to end up being part of a straight, two pairs, or trips (three of a kind) to win a big pot.

If there are a lot of opponents in the pot in front of you, and if you do hit a pair on the flop, there is a good chance that you will be out-kicked (an opponent will have a better kicker). For this reason, don't rely too heavily on them just because they are face cards (kings, queens, and jacks are called face cards). Fold them if the action has been raised and reraised in front of you.

A9s, A8s, A7s, A6s, A5s, A4s, A3s, A2s, K9s, QTs, JTs—With these hands you are hoping to flop a flush or flush draw. Rarely play these in any position except the button. Note that often the A9s through A6s are not as strong as A5s, A4, A3, and A2 since the latter can be part of a straight.

SMALL BLIND

The small blind is a unique situation in that you already have half a bet in the pot. This means that you can see the flop for a discounted price. For this reason, you will see the flop in an un-raised pot with any of the above hands and QT, JT, K8s, K7s, K6s, K5s, K4s, K3s, and K2s from the small blind. As in a few of the recommended hands above with the suited cards, you are hoping to flop a flush or flush draw and with the QT and JT a straight, straight draw, two pairs, or trips.

This is a good time to discuss the blinds. Once you have posted a blind, the money is no longer yours. Many players feel that because they have money in the pot, they must protect their blind. This thinking will often lead to playing far weaker hands than your opponents, and basically you will be throwing good money after bad. An example of this is if you are in the big blind and hold 2/7 unsuited.

A 2 and a 7 unsuited are the worst possible hole cards.

This is the worst possible starting hand. If the post is raised before you can act, you must fold. In a raised pot, you have such a minuscule chance of winning the hand with 2/7 that putting any more money in the pot will most often be costly. Another way to look at this is even if you had the opportunity to see the flop for free, you will rarely win a pot holding a hand as weak as 2/7.

You can also be psychologically trapped if the flop gives you a pair on one of your cards. Now, because you have a pair, you want to stay in the game, so you continue to throw money into the pot. In all probability, however, another player has your pair with a higher kicker because most players would not call the big blind with two low cards. If you hit two pairs, trips, or even a full house, the probability of you winning increases to the point where it would be worthwhile to continue, but the possibility of losing always looms.

It's easy for most players to release the worse possible hole cards when the prospect of winning is low, but what if your hole cards are J9 at the small blind, you call, and a J or an 8 and a 7 are flopped? You have a pair, and you have a chance at an inside straight. These types of hands can make you a loser in the long run if you stay with them against strong players. Remember, after the flop, you will be the first to bet—the worst possible position, so you have that against you as well. Using this same reasoning, don't call the half bet in the small blind without a decent starting hand.

BIG BLIND

When you are in the big blind, you will often have the opportunity to check and see the flop for free. This is usually a good play, especially if you hold a hand not mentioned above. There are, however, a few hands that you should raise with in the big blind. AA, KK, AKs, and AK should all be brought in with a raise to build the pot. An exception is if only one or two players have entered the pot, you may check with AA and KK in order to disguise your hand and give your opponents an opportunity to hit something on the flop. This can be dangerous because sometimes an opponent who limps in with a small pair may hit a set on the flop.

In this section we discussed the most important concept in becoming and staying a winning Hold 'Em player—starting hand selection. The hands listed are not the only hands you will ever play in Hold 'Em. As you gain experience and learn how certain opponents play and learn to read different situations, you will be able to play many different hands many different ways.

The important thing is to give yourself a fair chance to win or at least break even while gaining experience.

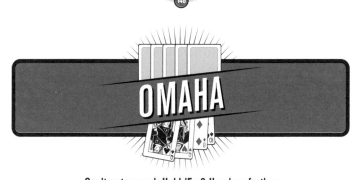

OMAHA

Can't get enough Hold 'Em? Here's a further
expanded version of the popular Poker game.

♣ ♦ ♠ ♥

PLAYERS

Three to eleven

PLAYING

For the basic rules, see Texas Hold 'Em. Deal four cards to each
player instead of two. In the showdown, use two cards in your
hand in combination with any three on the table. Often Omaha is
played high-low, which can attract a lot of betting action.

TIPS

With everyone holding four cards to the end, the caliber of winning hands rises. What you want, after the flop, is a clear winning
hand so good that it's a lock—no one could have a better hand
than yours. You want nothing to change this. But expect your
hopes to be dashed occasionally in this game—the two cards you
can't see may give someone else a better hand.

Here's an extreme case from high-low Omaha. You have ♣A-2-3, ♥A, and the flop is ♠A–5, ♦A. This looks too good to be true: You have four aces for high, and for low you have 2-3, the best possible low cards. So, you bet. The next card, is the ♦J, and you bet some more.

But the last card turned is the ♠3! All of a sudden, you have only a jack-low! Probably everyone has better. In fact, another player looking at ♠4-2 has made not only a perfect 5-low (wheel) but also has a lock on high—with a straight flush. After this hand, you'll be crying for a new deck, and for many weeks!

VARIATION

When played high-low, Omaha is one of several games where prevailing house rules can require that the low hand be an 8-low (e.g., 8-7-5-4-2) or better. If no one has an 8-low, the high hand takes the whole pot.

RUMMY

Rummy has been among America's most popular card games for decades. A 1930s survey determined that more Americans knew the rules for rummy than any other card game. Rummy is popular because it is easy to learn for people of all ages. And considering the many possible variations, you can always be playing a new and fun game.

♣ ♦ ♠ ♥

PLAYERS

Two to eight

OBJECT

To score points for melds or to stop the game when you're ahead in points.

CARDS

A regular pack of 52 cards is used.

BASICS

In most games, ten cards are dealt to each player. Play moves clockwise from the dealer's left. Players take turn drawing from stock, discarding, and building melds. Players try to be the first to deplete their hand of cards or to stop play (knock) when they have more points.

MELDS

Melds in Rummy consist of three or more cards of the same rank (♠4-♥4-♣4) or sequences of three or more cards in one suit (♣3-♣4-♣5).

KNOCKING

When one player ceases all play for a hand by verbalizing this word or by making the sound by rapping on the table.

Back in the 1930s, Gin was a minor branch of the Rummy family tree when suddenly Hollywood stars embraced it. Gin Rummy quickly became a national craze.

♣ ♦ ♠ ♥

PLAYERS

Two

OBJECT

To score more points than your opponent by melding your cards as quickly as possible.

CARDS

Standard 52-card deck. Aces are always low.

PLAYING

Draw high card to choose dealer. Ten cards are dealt to each player one at a time. The dealer starts the discard pile by turning one card faceup. This is the first upcard. The rest of the cards are placed facedown to serve as the stock. The opponent of the dealer has first refusal of the first upcard. If taken, the player then makes a discard. If refused, the dealer has the opportunity to take it. If neither player wants this card, the opponent draws the top card from the stock and discards.

Turns alternate. You may either take the top discard or the top card from the stock. Sort your cards into melds if you are able and then discard. If it is your turn, and you have taken a card, and all your cards except one card can be arranged into melds, say "Gin." Make your final discard facedown with that mismatched card, and put your hand faceup on the table.

Laying off is not allowed after gin is reached (see "Laying off" on the next page).

A gin hand is usually composed of three melds like this one, with one four-card meld and two three-card melds.

KNOCKING

You can also end play before your opponent reaches gin by "knocking." After picking up a card during your turn, discard a card facedown and rap on the table or say "Knock." You must place your melds faceup on the table and put your unmatched cards into a separate pile beside them. The unmatched cards are called "deadwood." Total deadwood points can't be greater than 10 points (see "Scoring" below for card values).

It is a good idea to plan a knock as early in the game as you can before your opponent has exchanged many cards from his/her hand. With a hand of ♥9-♥8-♥7-♥6-♥5-♠J-♦J-♣J-♦5-♥3, your deadwood adds up to 8 points—a score that your opponent might possibly beat late in the game. Thus, knocking isn't advisable in that situation.

LAYING OFF

If you knock, your opponent may lay off as many cards as possible onto the melds you've tabled. For example, you can lay off a ♣4 to a ♣7-♣6-♣5 run or a ♠Q to ♥Q-♣Q-♦Q set. This play reduces your opponent's count of deadwood.

SCORING

When tallying deadwood, aces count one point, face cards count 10 points, and all other cards are scored at face value.

If you gin, your score is the total of your opponent's deadwood points and a 25-point line bonus.

If you knock and your deadwood is less than your opponent's deadwood score, you receive the difference between the two deadwood scores.

If you knock and your opponent's deadwood count is equal to or lower than your deadwood count, your opponent receives a 20-point bonus for the "undercut," plus the difference in the deadwood scores.

If your opponent manages to lay off all unmelded cards, that player receives a 25-point bonus for "ginning off" and the difference in the deadwood scores.

The loser of a game deals the next hand. In a game in which two cards are remaining in the stock and no player knocks or can make gin, the hands are thrown in and no points are scored. The dealer then redeals. A fairly typical score for reaching gin is 100 points.

TIPS

Keep your cards in order; it makes it easier to determine melds. Gin is a game that rewards quick reflexes as well as a quick mind. Think ahead about discards. Don't play for gin when you think you can knock early.

VARIATIONS

Straight Gin is another popular gin game; it leaves out the knocking. For Gin Rummy for three or four players, there are multiple variations.

OKLAHOMA GIN

Oklahoma Gin is not the same card game as the one called "Oklahoma." Rather, it is an easy variation of regular Gin Rummy and is a favorite of many expert gin players.

♣ ♦ ♠ ♥

PLAYERS

Two

OBJECT

To meld your cards as quickly as possible.

CARDS

Standard 52-card deck. Aces are always low.

PLAYING

All of the rules of regular Gin Rummy apply, including scoring but excluding the knock rules. The first card turned up from the stock pile to form the discard pile determines the lowest count a player must have to knock.

VALUES FOR THE FIRST UPCARD

Ace	A gin hand is required to go out.
Face card or ten	10 points are required.
Any other card	The card's number or less. For example, a six requires six or less.

SCORING

Same as Gin Rummy, except when the upcard is a spade. Then, all scores except the line bonus are doubled for the hand.

You can't knock because the ♥4 and ♦4 in your hand are not melded and they total eight points, which is more than the first upcard—♣6.

GIN FOR THREE PLAYERS

The most common variation of Gin Rummy for three participants is Gin for Three Players. There are still only two players playing at a time, but all three players are involved trying to remain in play. It's basically a "winner stays" setup.

♣ ♦ ♠ ♥

PLAYERS

Three

OBJECT

To meld your cards as quickly as possible.

CARDS

Standard 52-card deck. Aces are always low.

PLAYING

Gin for Three Players uses the same rules as regular Gin Rummy. Each of the three players draws, with the player drawing the high card playing against the player drawing the second highest card. The high card player is said to be "in the box" while his/her opponent is called the "captain." The player drawing the low card sits out that game and remains silent. In the case of a tie or ties, draw until the tie is broken.

The captain deals. If the captain wins the game, that player then becomes the "in the box" player, the former "in the box" player sits out, with the player who sat out becoming captain in the next game. If the "in the box" player wins, that player remains in the box and the captain switches with the player who sat out.

SCORING

A running total is kept for each player, with scores accumulated over a set number of games. The first person to attain at least a predetermined number of points wins the game.

Also known as Pinochle Rummy, this fun game evolved into
several other favorite card games, such as Canasta.

♣ ♦ ♠ ♥

PLAYERS

Two to eight, but the game works best with three to five.

OBJECT

To score points for melds while discarding all your cards.

CARDS

For two to four players, use a standard 52-card deck. For five or
more players, use two standard 52-card decks (remember to use
decks that look the same on the back). Aces can be high or low.

PLAYING

For two players, deal ten cards each; for more players, deal seven
cards each. Count a meld by the value of the individual cards:
High aces count 15; low aces 1; face cards 10; and all other cards

count their face value. Unlike Gin Rummy, the discard pile is slightly spread so all cards can be seen.

Play begins to the dealer's left. Players may take the top card from the stock or any card in the discard pile—not just the top discard—on their turn as long as that card is immediately used in a meld or lay off. When you take a card from the discard pile, you must take all cards above the one you take. On the one hand, these extra cards provide additional opportunities to meld; on the other hand, they make it more difficult to go out. Place your melds on the table in front of you only after you draw a card and before you discard.

During a turn, players may also lay off cards to their own or other player's melds. Since these layoffs count toward your score, also keep the layoff cards in front of you on the table. A card can be laid off on another layoff card. Thus, if an ♣8 is laid off a meld of a ♣7-♣6-♣5, a ♣9 can be laid off on the ♣8. Sequences cannot "go round the corner"—that is, if either a high or low ace is used in a sequence, a layoff card cannot be used off of the ace. Thus, a 2 cannot be laid off on an A-K-Q sequence, nor can a K be laid off on an A-2-3 sequence.

The player of these melds will want to count the aces in the set as high but will have to count the ace in the run as low.

The game is over when a player goes out by melding or laying off all his/her cards. No final discard is needed. If no one goes out, the game ends when the stock runs out.

SCORING

Players total their melds and lay offs, then subtract the value of the cards left in their hand. No bonus points are awarded for going out. If the points left in a player's hand exceed the points on the table, that number of points is subtracted from that player's overall score. A player can have a negative score.

The first player to score 500 points or more wins the game. If more than one player exceeds 500 at the end of a hand, the player with the most points wins the game.

TIPS

Try to make melds with high-scoring cards if you can. The visibility of face cards in the discard pile allows you to make more strategic discards and picks.

KNOCK RUMMY

This card game is fun for mixed groups of children and adults.

♣ ♦ ♠ ♥

PLAYERS

Two to five (Six players are possible, but that number of players reduces the amount of play.)

OBJECT

To knock and stop play when your count of deadwood is less than that of your opponents.

CARDS

Standard 52-card deck. Aces are low.

DEALING

With two players, deal 10 cards each. With three and four players, deal 7 cards each. For five and six players, deal 6 cards each.

PLAYING

Knock Rummy plays like Gin Rummy, except that players do not have to gin to stop play. Any player can knock. Unlike Gin Rummy, the knocker's deadwood does not have to be less than 10 points. A player knocks after drawing the top card from the stock or the top card from the discard pile and before discarding. The knocker then discards, and all players show their cards, separating melds and unmatched cards. Cards are not laid off.

SCORING

If you knock and have the lowest deadwood count, you win the point difference from all other players. If you knock and rummy (that is, all your cards are used in melds), you receive the point difference and a 25-point bonus from each opponent. If you knock and an opponent has the same amount of deadwood points, that opponent collects the point difference from the other players. If more than one opponent ties your deadwood score, they split the difference. If you knock and one or more opponents have less deadwood points, the opponent with the lowest score receives the point difference from each player. If they tie, they split the difference.

Every opponent who has less deadwood points than you also receives a 10-point penalty from you. Before the first hand, players determine the score needed to win the game.

TIPS

Approach the game differently depending on how many people are playing. The fewer the players, the higher your deadwood count can be when you knock. For example, an early knock with under 30 points when playing with one opponent is usually safe. With four or more players, the added bonus of 25 points for gin may make waiting with an initial meld worthwhile. If your deadwood count is low, however, don't wait too long; an opponent may draw enough cards to knock and win.

Player B knocks and then discards. He has two melds of 4s and 7s, with one deadwood card—♦6, which is 6 points. Player C has one meld of four 2s with three deadwood cards—♠3, ♥A, and ♦A, which is 5 points. Thus, Player C receives a 10-point penalty from Player B, plus a 1 point difference and a 17 point difference with Player A for a total of 28 points.

SLAPJACK

This fast-paced card game is perfect for the whole family to enjoy.

♣ ♦ ♠ ♥

PLAYERS

Two to eight

OBJECT

To win all of the cards.

CARDS

Slapjack is normally played with a single 52-card deck of standard playing cards, but there is no limit to the number of decks that can be used. The game lasts longer and is more fun for everyone involved if more decks are added as the number of players increases. The game can get pretty wild as more players join the game and usually leads to a fun time for all. There is a good chance that the playing cards will be damaged or bent during game play (especially the jacks), so it is recommended that older decks are used.

PLAYING

Start the game by choosing a dealer. To do this, shuffle the cards and deal one card faceup to each player. The player with the highest card is the dealer for the first game. After each game, the deal passes one player to the left. The dealer reshuffles the cards and deals them all out, one at a time, facedown, starting with the player to the left. Players keep their cards facedown in a single stack in front of them. Starting with the player to the dealer's left, players in turn flip the top card from their pile faceup onto the common stack in the center of the table. This continues until a jack is turned faceup.

When a jack is played to the center of the table, players try to be the first to slap the jack with their open palm. Whoever is first to slap the jack takes all of the cards from the center pile and places them facedown at the bottom of their stack. Depending on how many players start the game and how many decks of cards are used, a game of Slapjack can last for hours.

Here are a few additional rules that need to be strictly enforced to make the game fair and fun for everyone. For starters, each player must turn cards up from their facedown pile away from them so they cannot cheat by seeing their card before any of the other players. Also, players must use the same hand they turn cards over with to slap jacks. This keeps players from hovering over the pile. To keep arguments to minimum, there are no ties. When more than one player slaps a jack, the hand at the bottom of the pile wins. Finally, any player who slaps a card that is not a jack must place one card from his/her pile at the bottom of the center stack as a penalty.

SPADES

This bidding game is a favorite with soldiers in the U.S. military. Each branch of service seems to have its own special version. There are also plenty of regional variations, as well as two-, three-, and five-handed games. The rules given here are for the four-handed partnership version of the game.

♣ ♦ ♠ ♥

PLAYERS

Four play as fixed pairs. You may either choose your partner or draw from a deck to determine partners. Partners sit opposite each other.

OBJECT

To win the number of tricks that your side bids.

CARDS

Use a standard 52-card deck. Aces are high. Score pads are helpful.

DEALING

Drawing the high card from downcards determines who deals first. Each player is then dealt 13 cards. The deal proceeds clockwise.

BIDDING

Play begins after a single round of bids. Every player must make a bid of at least one trick; there are no passes, and no suit is named to be trump since spades are always trump. Bidding begins from the dealer's left.

After each player makes a bid, both partners combine their bids to total their contract bids. It does not matter who wins the tricks as long as the team makes the contract. Here's an example: The player on your left bids three, your partner also bids three, the next player bids four, and you bid two. This means that your opponents' contract is to take seven tricks while your team's contract is to win five tricks. It's a good idea to write down the bids.

It isn't always good strategy to play a trump if you can't follow suit. If you have a short suit, like these diamonds, use them up quickly. Your partner can then lead to your void suit giving you a better use for your trumps.

PLAYING

The player at dealer's left leads but cannot lead a spade (trump) for the first trick. The play moves clockwise. You must follow the suit led. If you cannot follow suit, play any card. You do not have to play a trump unless it is the led suit. The highest card of the led suit wins the trick unless a spade trumps the trick. If more than one trump is played in a trick, the highest trump wins. A spade can be played only if the player has no cards in the led suit. A spade cannot be led until a spade has "trumped" an earlier trick or when only spades are left in the hand.

The winner of a trick leads to the next trick. Cards in a trick should be piled together in a stack visible to all players. Each pile should have some separation so tricks can be counted during and after play. This simplifies score keeping. If a player does not follow suit while holding unplayed cards of that suit, that partnership cannot score any points even if they make their contract.

SCORING

Prior to the first hand, players decide on what score is needed to win. This score is usually a multiple of 100; 500 is customary. If you make your contract, multiply the number of tricks by 10 for the total trick points. Each trick you win above your contract, called a "sandbag," counts for 1 point. If you fail to make your contract, you lose 10 points for every trick bid.

For example, your side bids eight, and your opponents bid four. Your side wins ten tricks, and their side wins three tricks. Your side scores 82 points (successful contract of eight, plus two sandbags); your opponents lose 40 points (failing to make contract of four tricks).

SANDBAGS

Don't think that overtricks are good for your bottom line. Under-bids work against you. As soon as your sandbags total ten, 100 points are subtracted from your total score (besides the running score, also track the number of sandbags separately). If you have more than ten sandbags, leftovers begin a new count toward ten. For example, you bid four and win six tricks. If you already have nine sandbags, you will be penalized 100 points and have one sandbag toward the next count of ten. Penalties for sandbags help discourage underbidding.

TIPS

Flushing out the trumps is a great strategy for Spades. When you lead a low trump, your opponents must follow suit and thereby waste their trump cards.

Once you become comfortable with the basic bid rules of Spades, try some high-scoring variations like the ones below.

TEN FOR TWO

The first partner to bid declares a contract for ten tricks without their partner's help. A successful bid gives the team double the points. Thus, a successful ten bid nets 200 points, but a failed ten bid only has 100 points deducted. In addition, no points are awarded for overtricks.

NIL BID

In order to make a "nil" bid, partners must be losing by at least 100 points. The player who bids nil indicates they won't win any tricks. The successful nil bid nets 50 points, but if you fail, you lose 50 points. Only one member of a partnership can make a nil bid. The partner's bid becomes the number of tricks that partner must win alone. If the nil bidder wins a trick, that trick cannot count toward the partner's bid. Both the nil bid and the partner's bid are tallied together.

BLIND NIL

Similar to nil except the nil bidder cannot look at their cards before bidding. If successful, 100 points are earned, but if unsuccessful, 100 points are deducted. With a blind nil bid, partners of this bid may exchange two cards after they look at their cards but before play begins.

This is an excellent "nil" hand. Several low hearts protect the high hearts. The high hearts can also be thrown away on club leads.

Speed (also known as Spit) is a fast-paced
card game that is fun for everyone.

♣ ♦ ♠ ♥

PLAYERS

Two

OBJECT

Be the first person to play all of your cards. Speed is normally
played in a best-of-three series, but it can also be played as a
single game.

CARDS

Use a standard 52-card deck of playing cards.

PLAYING

After the cards are shuffled, each player receives half of the deck
(26 cards). Each player then creates a stack of 15 cards (the

draw pile) and places it facedown to the front and right. Each player also has a 5-card hand. In front of the stack of 15 cards is a facedown stack of 5 cards (the replacement pile), and the final card is placed to the left of the replacement pile facedown. These two single cards, one for each player, end up side-by-side in the center of the table.

Each player flips his/her single card in the center of the table faceup at the same time. Then, each player plays one card at a time as fast as possible from his/her hand. After you play a card from your hand, you take a new card from your draw pile. Cards can be played on either of the two stacks in the center of the table and can be in sequence up or down.

Suits are ignored in Speed. For example, if a 4 is on top of one of the stacks, a 3 or a 5 can be played on top of it. Aces go around the corner to kings or deuces. When both players have five cards in their hand and neither can make an additional play, each player simultaneously flips the top card from his/her replacement piles onto the center stacks to start again.

A player may play more than one card in succession on either stack, but he/she must do so one at a time. That player may not play, for example, a 5, 6, and 7 at one time, but he/she may place the 5, then the 6, and finally the 7 individually.

If all of the cards are used up before one of the players has won, the two center stacks are shuffled and used as new replacement stacks.

The facedown pile at the top is flipped by the player on the right, and the pile at the bottom is flipped by the player on the left. With the cards shown here, you could play a 2 or K on the A or a 4 or 6 on the 5.

VARIATIONS

There are a wide variety of options and house rules for Speed. It seems as though everyone plays a little bit differently depending on where they learned how to play, so make sure both players understand and agree on the rules before the game starts. The doubles rule allows you to play the same card on the two stacks, instead of just being able to play the next higher or lower card.

For example, on a stack with an 8 on the top, players may play a 7, 8, or 9. You can also play with four-card hands. With this rule, players keep four cards in their hands instead of five. In this method, the draw pile is set at 16 cards at the beginning of the hand.

Some games also play with jokers. The two jokers are left in the deck and can be played at any time. When a joker is played, it must be declared. In other words, the player who puts down the joker must state for what card it is being used. In another variation, the joker does not have to be named, and any card can be played on it. When using jokers, the draw pile is set at 16 cards instead of 15 at the beginning of the game—17 if using four-card hands.

SPOONS

Spoons is an exciting party game that's easy to learn and suitable for all ages. No matter what your skill level, this is fast-paced family fun!

♣ ♦ ♠ ♥

PLAYERS

Two to eight

OBJECT

Be the first to get four of a kind.

CARDS

A standard 52-card deck of playing cards and spoons (or other easy-to-grab objects) are needed to play. There should be one fewer spoon than the number of players. So if there are five players, you need four spoons.

PLAYING

A dealer is chosen at random and deals out four cards to each player. The rest of the cards are placed facedown next to the dealer. The dealer begins by picking up a card from the pile and deciding whether or not to keep it. If he/she chooses not to keep it, the card is passed facedown to the player to the left. If that player keeps the card, a card from his/her hand must be passed to the next player, since only four cards are allowed in a hand at any given time. This process repeats for each player around the table.

The last player in the rotation creates a discard pile next to the dealer, which can be used by the dealer if cards run out in the original pile.

Once you get four of a kind, quickly and quietly pick up a spoon while continuing to pass cards. Once others notice that a spoon has been taken, they can also pick up spoons. The last player without a spoon loses and sits out the next round and one spoon is removed from the table. You can continue playing in this fashion until there is a final winner.

If you are passed the ♣2, it would be a good idea to keep it and pair it with your ♦2. You can then choose any of your other cards to pass.

VARIATION

You can make the game last longer by assigning the loser of each round a letter in the word "SPOONS" instead of eliminating that person from play immediately. For example, if a player loses the first round, they would be assigned the letter S. Once the word is completed for any player, then that player must leave the game. In this version, some people prefer to keep a score sheet in order to keep track of each player's letters.

TWENTY-ONE

Don't confuse this game with the casino game of Blackjack, also called 21. Even children can play this easy-to-learn numbers game, and anyone can win!

♣ ♦ ♠ ♥

PLAYERS

Two to seven

OBJECT

To win as many cards as possible without going over 21.

CARDS

A regular pack of 52 cards is used. Aces and picture cards count 1 point each, all others count their face value.

PLAYING

Deal the cards out equally, and set aside any remaining cards. Starting at dealer's left and continuing clockwise around the table, players build a card count up to 21. As each card is played the new total is announced.

When you play a card that reaches 21 exactly, collect the cards in the center. However, when any card you have would go over 21, say "Stop." The player on your right collects the cards. The player who said "Stop," begins the next count toward 21 The hand is over when the final player gathers in the last cards.

SCORING

Players count the cards they've won, each card counting 1 point. The first player to 50 points (or any other agreed-upon total) wins.

TIP

A usual strategy for most players is to play their high-count cards early. This leads to more low cards in the later rounds, and so the center pile tends to be bigger after the first few build to 21.

VARIATIONS

You can play this game blind, with each player turning up a card from a pile at each turn without knowing its value.

The count has gone 6-14-15-19. If you have a 2, you can score 21 exactly and
win the cards. If you have an ace or a picture card, you can still play. Otherwise, say, "Stop." The player on your right gathers in the cards, and you begin a new count.

WAR

Along with Old Maid, War is one of the first card games children learn to play. In practical terms, it rarely ends with a thorough defeat.

♣ ♦ ♠ ♥

PLAYERS

Two or more

OBJECT

To win all the cards.

CARDS

Use a regular pack of 52 cards. Aces are high.

PLAYING

Divide the pack equally into facedown piles for each player. At the same time, each player turns over their top card. Whoever has the higher card wins both cards, and the process is repeated. Place the cards you win on the bottom of your pile.

Occasionally, both players turn up cards of the same rank. This starts a war, in which each player lays three more cards facedown, then turns up the next card. Whoever's card is higher wins all the cards from the war. If the cards tie again, lay three more cards facedown and then turn the next card up to determine the winner.

The game ends when one player takes all the cards. You can try a shorter game, where you go through the cards just once or twice, and then see who has won the most cards.

VARIATION

For three or more players, deal the cards out as equally as possible. Turn cards as before, and when players tie for best card, each plays two more facedown cards, with the next card turned up to decide a winner. Players not in the war must also contribute their next three cards. Play continues until one player has all the cards.

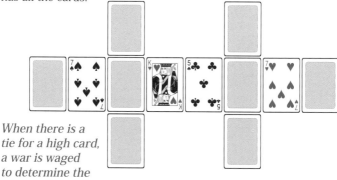

When there is a tie for a high card, a war is waged to determine the winner. Here, players were tied at 7, and the player with the K is the winner of this war.

WHIST

Some might consider this ancestor of Bridge and other games to be obsolete. Nonetheless, even today Whist offers a nice combination of luck, skill, and surprise.

♣ ♦ ♠ ♥

PLAYERS

Four, in pairs with partners facing each other.

OBJECT

To win a majority of the 13 tricks.

CARDS

A regular deck of 52 cards is used. By custom, dealer's partner shuffles a second deck for the other side to use on the following hand.

PLAYING

Deal 13 cards to each player, with the last card dealt face up to designate the trump suit. Player at dealer's left leads any card, and dealer, before playing to the first trick, picks up the turned-up card. Whenever possible, players follow suit but otherwise may play any card, including a trump. A trick is won by the highest trump card in it or else by the highest card played of the suit led. The winner of each trick leads to the next trick.

SCORING

The side taking the majority of tricks scores 1 point for each trick won over six. For example, a side that wins 10 of 13 tricks scores 4. Game goes to the first side to reach 10 points or any other agreed-upon number.

TIPS

In order to win the majority of tricks, you must do more than take tricks with aces—you must try to make winners out of lower cards. For example, ♦s are trump and your hand includes ♣Q-J-10. Even when the opponents have both ♣A and ♣K, if you can lead ♣ twice, you establish a high card in the suit. Even if your ♣s are Q-9-6-4, lead the ♣4, and see what happens. If partner has some high clubs, you may together be able to make the ♣Q high to win a trick later.

In general, at the start of play, when you are long in trumps (4 or more cards), lead another long suit if you have one. When you have a short trump holding (2 or fewer), lead another short suit.

WHISTLET

This game appears to be a compact form of German Whist. Simple to play, Whistlet supplies an engaging mix of luck and skill. And you can learn to play in about one minute.

♣ ◆ ♠ ♥

PLAYERS

Two

OBJECT

To win the most tricks.

CARDS

A regular pack of 52 cards is used. Aces are high.

PLAYING

Deal seven cards to each player, one at a time. Turn the next card over and place it face up next to the stock. The suit of this card will be the trump suit.

Nondealer leads to the first trick. You must follow suit when you are able to; otherwise, trump or discard. A trick is won by the higher trump in it or, if it contains no trump, by the higher card of the suit led. After each trick, both players take a new card from the stock. The winner of the trick draws first and leads to the next trick.

Each deal consists of 26 tricks. The last seven tricks are played after the stock pile is gone. Winner of the 19th trick draws the remaining stock card; the loser takes the trump upcard. Keep track of individual tricks each player has won.

SCORING

The player who took the greater number of tricks scores the difference between that number and the lesser number of tricks. If both players took 13 tricks, neither scores; but if one player took 15 tricks and the other took 11, the winner scores 4 points.

TIPS

Even if you are void in a suit, use judgment in trumping. It may be better strategy to shed a loser by discarding it.

In the last seven tricks, it will pay to have more trumps than your opponent.

In the illustration, suppose spades are trump. With the last seven tricks to go, you should play the left hand by leading any spade in your hand until your opponent is forced to play the king. After regaining the lead, draw opponent's remaining trumps by leading a winning spade each time. Then the rest of your cards are winners, too.

The trump suit contains exactly 13 cards. If you keep count of the trumps played, you'll know in the endgame just how many trumps your opponent has. As in most games, the better you remember the cards that have been played, the better you'll do. Keeping track of trumps and a few high cards is helpful, but if you can remember every card in the first part of the game, you'll know your opponent's last seven cards.

In the first phase of play, you may well discover opponent to be void of a suit. It may be a good risk to continue leading that suit, when your objective is to reduce your opponent's trumps. If your objective instead is to win your low trumps, then it may pay to lead a singleton, hoping to remain void in that suit later.

VARIATION

Play Whistlet just as above, but try to lose as many tricks as possible. When you must win a trick, use the highest card available. At the end of play, the one with fewer tricks scores the points.

GLOSSARY

BID

A spoken declaration to win a specified number of tricks or points; also, to make such a declaration.

CONTRACT

An agreement to win a certain number of tricks or points in a game or round.

CUTTHROAT

Each player playing on his or her own.

DEAL

The act of portioning out the cards to the players; also, the period of play in the game between one deal and the next.

DECLARATION

A statement to fulfill a contract.

DEUCE

A card of the rank of two; also called a two-spot.

DRAW TRUMPS

To lead high trumps in order to deplete opponent's hand of trumps.

DRAW

To take a new card or cards.

FACE CARD

A king, queen, or jack.

FACE VALUE

The numerical value of a card.

FLUSH

A set of cards all of the same suit.

FOLLOW SUIT

To play a card of the suit led.

GAME

A total number of points to achieve; also, what constitutes winning or ending a game.

GOING OUT

Playing, melding, or discarding your final card.

HAND

The cards dealt to a player; also, the period of play in the game between one deal and the next.

KITTY

A common chip pool; also (in a few games) cards available for exchange.

LAY OFF

To play one or more cards according to allowable plays.

LEAD

To play the first card to a trick.

MAKER

A player who takes on a specific obligation, such as to take a certain number of points or tricks, often along with the right to choose the trump suit.

MARRIAGE

A meld consisting of the king and queen.

MATCH

To equate by being of the same rank (or by another criterion).

MELD

A combination of cards with scoring value, generally three or more cards in sequence in one suit or all of the same rank; also, to show or play such a combination.

NO-TRUMP

The condition when no suit is trumps in a trick-taking game.

PASS

A spoken declaration not to make a bid; in Hearts, three hidden cards exchanged among the players.

PLAIN CARD

Any 10, 9, 8, 7, 6, 5, 4, 3, 2, or ace.

SEQUENCE

Two or more cards in consecutive order.

SINGLETON

A holding of only one card in a suit.

STOCK

The undealt cards available for future use.

TABLE

The playing area; also, to lay down a meld on the playing area.

TALON

A portion of the pack reserved for later use during the deal.

TRICK

A round of cards played, one from each player's hand.

TRUMP

A suit designated to be higher ranking than any other suit; any card in that suit. Also, to play a trump card on a trick.

UPCARD

The first card turned up after a deal, often to begin play or initiate a discard pile.

VOID

A lack of a suit in a player's hand.

WILD CARD

A card or cards, established before the game begins, that can be designated by the holder to stand for any other card.